REST MATTERS

Listening to the heartbeat of Jesus

LIN BUTTON

Published by HPS Publishing, Essex, United Kingdom

First Edition 2025

ISBN: 978-0-9567093-4-9

Cover: painting by Randall Staley

To the HPS team.
We have prayed, laughed, eaten and celebrated together
for the last five years, finding rest in our souls by being
together.

To Simon, Justine and Dominic for all their love, care and
support

Acknowledgements

To my family:

Sons, daughter-in-law, grandchildren; All Saints Woodford Wells Church; Monday Group; HPS Team – all family in different ways.

Special thanks to:

Linda and David Crawley, Gini Crompton, Pamela Evans and Randall Staley, for reading and giving me helpful feedback.

Randall Staley for the painting which became the cover of this book.

Linda and David Crawley for making the draft pages become a book.

Vivienne Stockley who began the typing during lockdown and then on retirement as my administrator handed over the administration job, as well as the typing and retyping, to Becky Harcourt.

Canon Rev Paul Harcourt for guiding our church throughout all of the changes of the last five years.

Contents

INTRODUCTION

Back in July 2019, in my prayer time I kept seeing a picture of a giant hamster wheel. As I looked at it, I thought, "That is most people's lifestyle, not just in the world but in the Church also." With that, I knew the title of my next book, "Rest Matters".

In December, I planned talks all around rest for a seminar series and as the theme for the 2020 five-day healing prayer conference. Then Covid-19 and lockdown came, and I thought I must have it wrong because no-one would need to learn about rest, as we were all about to experience an enforced rest! I said this to a friend, who replied, "No, some will be involved immediately in other activities like making banana bread! Others will not be at rest due to anxiety and fear about the virus – (they soon learned not to watch every news item) – and others will be busier than now, juggling the responsibilities of children, jobs or elderly parents." So, I went ahead!

I really believe Matthew 11:28 (TPT): *"Are you weary, carrying a heavy burden? Then come to Me. I will refresh your life, for I am your oasis."*

The western world is busy not just at work but with an ever-increasing social life. The church needs to be different, demonstrating a better way to live, without adding more events to an overfull diary. Whilst I was writing this book, John Mark Comer's book *The Ruthless Elimination of Hurry* was published and I read Walter Bruggeman's book *Sabbath Resistance.*

What I want to explore in this book is rest from the inside – our internal landscape – and how rest is linked to connectedness. Being drastic with our diaries and lifestyle choices will help, but we need a transformation of our hearts to truly experience rest and peace.

Chapter 1

ENTERING GOD'S REST

There are different Greek words all translated as 'rest' which have different meanings. One word means 'to lean upon' or 'to trust in something or someone'.

Another word means the permanent rest of the eternal Kingdom.

A different Greek word is used by Jesus in Matthew 11:28, *"Come to me, all you who are weary and burdened, and I will give you rest"*, which is the type of rest we are to have in this life to keep us from getting stressed. If we over-extend ourselves, this can be to our physical, emotional and spiritual detriment.

Therefore, rest is linked not just with the idea of stopping work 'to have a little rest' but with the idea of living in the perfect harmony of God's presence; His shalom –wholeness, peace – His 'unforced rhythms of grace' Matthew 11:28-30 (MSG). God gave us the gift of Sabbath rest.

I used to misunderstand these words. When I was first a Christian – as a boundary-less, 'wanting to belong' church member, I said yes to everything and was very busy! Two good Christian friends kept telling me I needed to rest. Therefore, when my husband and I went on our annual seaside holiday with our two boys, my eldest boy wanted to play tennis, which I loved, but I said no, believing I had to rest. They all went for long walks along the water's edge but I stayed firmly in my deckchair, resting. I had a thoroughly miserable time! My friends had correctly discerned something was wrong but were not skilled, experienced or mature enough to recognise the underlying issue. A short-change of lifestyle was not the answer, and the fact that I had more energy and capacity than most people was another confusing ingredient!

Unfortunately, in some UK churches, the Sabbath has come to mean 'Sunday best' and the banning of anything pleasurable. I believe this to be a travesty of God's original intention. Many years ago, my husband Ron and I were in Israel, and during one part of the holiday we were staying on a kibbutz during Shabbat. We noticed that when we went to bed, a plaster had been stuck over the buttons to the lift and the next morning, at breakfast, a tea towel had been placed over the toaster. Apparently, this was because no electricity was to be used. Now, we can think, "How ridiculous, how silly, what sort of religion teaches that?!"

But those people weren't bad or silly. They were doing their best to obey the Law (the Torah) and to please God according to their understanding. The deeper, more disturbing thought is, what sort of God – what image of God – did they have which led them to believe He would be pleased with a tea towel draped over a toaster? They were living with a list of rules and regulations, presumably because they believed it would keep God happy.

Matthew 12:1-2: *"At that time Jesus went through the grain fields on the Sabbath. His disciples were hungry and began to pick some heads of grain and eat them. When the Pharisees saw this, they said to him, 'Look! Your disciples are doing what is unlawful on the Sabbath.'"*

The Pharisees had established thirty-nine general categories of actions forbidden on the Sabbath based on interpretations of God's law and on Jewish customs. Harvesting was one of those forbidden actions. By picking wheat and rubbing it in their hands, the disciples were technically harvesting, according to the religious leaders. Jesus and the disciples were picking grain because they were hungry, not because they wanted to harvest the grain for a profit. Jesus and the disciples were not working on the Sabbath. The Pharisees, however, could not (and did not want to) see beyond the Law's technicalities. They had no room for compassion and were determined to accuse Jesus of wrongdoing. They cried out, *'Your disciples are breaking the Sabbath rules!'* Jesus retorted by reminding them of the story of David recorded in 1 Samuel 21:1-6 when David went to the priest, disguised the fact that he was on the run from Saul, and asked for food. The priest gave him bread he would not normally be allowed to eat.

The Bread of the Presence was replaced every week, and the old loaves were eaten by the priests. The loaves given to David were the old loaves that had just been replaced with fresh ones. Although the priests were the only ones allowed to eat the bread, God did not punish David because his need for food was more important than the legal technicalities. Jesus was saying, "If you condemn me, you must also condemn David," something the religious leaders could never do without causing a great uproar among the people. Jesus says, *"And didn't you ever read in God's law that priests carrying out their temple duties break Sabbath rules all the time and it's not held against them? There is far more at stake here than religion. If you had any idea what this scripture meant, 'I prefer a flexible heart to an inflexible ritual' you wouldn't be nitpicking like this."* Matthew 12:4 (MSG)

Jeremiah 7:21-23, paraphrased, reads, "I don't want your sacrifices – I didn't ask for them – but live the way I tell you and your lives will go well", and, let's be honest, often we are no different to the Pharisees. We prefer a map to a guide, we prefer law to a relationship, and we have a distorted image of God whereby we believe we have to keep Him happy by being good or nice. Our false image of God causes us to live a life of performance, adhering to rules and regulations, 'oughts' and 'shoulds', or, as Dallas Willard calls it, 'a life of sin management'.

When we have a false image of God this affects how we see God which, in turn, affects how we see ourselves and others. Jesus says to Philip in John 14:9, *"Anyone who has seen me has seen the Father." "To see Me is to see the Father."* (MSG) When I first became a Christian, I couldn't understand why the Pharisees couldn't see who Jesus was. Why were they so blind? Now I pray, "Don't let me be blind to who Jesus is", because we can so easily accumulate a series of 'tick boxes' of how Jesus should and shouldn't behave! When we live like this, we miss both Jesus and the Sabbath. Quoting Tim Keller, "The word, 'Sabbath' means 'a deep rest, a deep peace.'[1] It's linked to shalom – a state of wholeness and flourishing in every dimension of life. When Jesus says, 'I am the Lord of the Sabbath', Jesus means that He *is* the Sabbath; He is the source of the deep rest we need. This new life He brings changes everything, including the way we think about rest. The one-day-a-week rest we take is just a taste of the deep, divine rest we need, and Jesus is its source. When Jesus says, in effect, 'As the Lord of the Sabbath, I can give you rest', what does that mean? When Jesus calls you to rest, He is calling you to take time off – physically and mentally – on a regular basis. But there's another level of rest, a deeper level."[2]

The beginning of Chapter two of Genesis states, "God rested from His work". I don't think this is because He was tired and worn out but more that He rested in the goodness of what He had created. He blessed it and declared it holy, and what if – just a thought – He wanted to spend time with Adam and Eve? Now, because of all the distortions and petty lifestyle rules, I (like many others) threw out the concept of Sabbath in any meaningful way. Walter Brueggemann in his book "Sabbath Resistance" argues powerfully for the reinstatement of the Sabbath from the position of understanding the deeper meaning of the ten commandments in Exodus. John Mark Comer, in his book "The Ruthless Elimination of Hurry", comes to much the same conclusion. After experiencing burnout, he chose a change of lifestyle for himself and for his family that incorporates Sabbath.

In July 2019, I started to think about rest and this book, having observed my working sons' somewhat frenetic lifestyles, often mirrored in busy churches. I began small and simply decided that for 24 hours during a week I would not look at emails, the internet or texts. I have continued in this. In the late winter of 2020, I read both the above books, finishing one of them at the beginning of lockdown.

The ancient Greeks saw the pursuit of leisure as a virtue.[3] To them, leisure did not mean a self-indulgent, narcissistic lifestyle, nor was it idleness. It meant pursuing that which resulted in joy and meaning (we are more likely to use the word 'play'). Dr Stuart Brown, a psychiatrist, clinical researcher and founder of the National Institute for Play, draws on his own research, as well as on the latest advances in biology, psychology and neurology. Brown explains that play shapes our brain, helps us foster empathy, helps us navigate complex social groups and is at the core of creativity and innovation. If you are wondering why I am writing about play in a Chapter on rest, it is because I believe play is part of rest. Remember me on holiday denying myself the pleasure of playing with my family?

What is play? Play may involve doing something we want to do which appears purposeless. If our self-worth and identity is in achievement, this can feel like a waste of time. We have got to 'get it done', whatever *it* is, otherwise we might view ourselves as lazy. We can think, "This is no time to be playing around." Dr Brown argues not playing is not an option. He writes, "*The opposite of play is not* work, *the opposite of play is* depression".[4] Brené Brown writes in her book, "*If you must write a list it should be headed, 'Ingredients for Joy and Meaning'*".[5]

Before I write more on rest, I want to explore the word 'stress'. It appears that these days it is alright to be stressed because, somehow, it has come to be expected that life is stressful, that certain circumstances are stressful. That isn't the issue though. The issue is how to respond to the stress. It also feels less shameful to admit to ourselves that we are stressed rather than to be fearful or anxious. Dr Pamela Evans speaks of how in some circles it's a badge of honour. "I am stressed" means I am important, doing important things.

So often we are stressed, fearful or anxious because of our tight fists of control. This is counterfeit and illusory, of course, because so much of what we try to control (thereby losing our rest) is *outside* of our control or not ours to control! Trust is the antithesis of stress: "*The joys of those who trust the Lord,*" Psalm 40:4 (NLT). The Greek word *pisteuo* appears 200 times in the New Testament. It means 'belief 'or 'faith'. It ultimately means to put one's faith in, to trust, to rest on. In order to live in rest, we need to cultivate a faith that deeply trusts.

John 6:28-29 (AMPC): *"They then said, 'What are we to do, that we may [habitually] be working the works of God? [What are we to do to carry out what God requires?'] Jesus replied, 'This is the work (service) that God asks of you: that you believe in the One Whom He has sent, [that you cleave to, trust, rely on and have faith in His Messenger].'"*

What's my daily work, the work God asks of me? To trust and let go of control. In Song of Songs Chapter 4:8, we are invited through the archway of trust (TPT), in Hebrew the 'crest of Amana', from which we get the word 'amen' in English and many other languages, where all God's promises are kept and realized. A place of settled security.

Yet our old, established neural pathways go straight to stress, worry and anxiety. New pathways are unknown and arduous even though they lead to grace, joy and thanksgiving. Sometimes it all feels like too much energy and, after all, stress and anxiety are familiar. It's easy to let our imaginations run wild with fear and worry rather than put boundaries around our thoughts and cultivate rest. As we trust, we learn to open our hands and let go:

- Letting go of trying to compensate and fix the past.
- Letting go of worry about or control of partners, adult children or work colleagues.
- Letting go of fear of the words of others.
- Letting go of trying to work everything out.
- Letting go of worry.
- Letting go of fear of the future.

You will have your own "letting go's".

Extract from my diary, Monday 21st October 2012:

REST: Had picture in a staff meeting when we sang, *'This is the Rock on which I stand, all other ground is shifting sand'*. The picture is of someone on a rock surrounded by swamp and quicksand. The person is standing on the edge of a rock trying to reach out to Jesus, who is on the other side of the picture. But the person is frightened of falling off. God said just sit down in the centre of the rock. When the person did, it became 'Disney-like'; green grass rolled out around the rock and flowers sprang up. Rest is the sword against anxiety, and rest in the Bible is linked with presence. We sit not cross-armed, passive, but with confident expectation.

In Exodus 33, we read of Moses asking God what to do. In verse 14, God answers, *"My presence will go with you and I will give you rest."* In Psalm 62:1-2 (NRSV), we read, *"For God alone my soul waits in silence. From Him comes my salvation. He alone is my rock and salvation. My fortress. I shall never be shaken."*

When we are anxious, all this feels impossible. We may feel on the edge of the rock, striving for healing; striving for the answer. Rest feels scary. Someone said to me the other day, "I'm okay if I keep busy; I'm okay if I keep going." Our difficulty is we believe that if we stop, if we rest, all those anxious thoughts will overwhelm us. This may be because we associate rest with stopping and being on our own; whereas God given rest on the inside is linked with God's presence. Again, this may be difficult for us to comprehend. We suffer from restless activity, maybe not in what we do, but in our heads. The mental chatter, the internal busyness we use to smother feelings of anxiety.

We also have a temptation to fix ourselves. Isaiah 50:10-11 (NLT): *"Who among you fears the Lord and obeys His servant? If you are walking in darkness, without a ray of light, trust in the Lord and rely on your God. But watch out, you who live in your own light and warm yourselves by your own fires. This is the reward you will receive from me; You will soon lie down in great torment."* Our inner life can be like a troubled sea, where it cannot rest. We need to ask ourselves, "What keeps me awake at night? What owns me? What drives me? Am I continually anxious, burdened and overwhelmed?"

Clay McLean speaks of the place of rest being the place where eternity visits us and we visit eternity.[6] See how the following words from Jeremiah challenge your belief system, your faith and your lifestyle. Just think of the lies and evil reports you have listened to, times when you've paid more attention to worldly views over and above God's word. Now take in *these* words from Jeremiah and examine your heart to see if your way of living reflects this:

Jeremiah 29:11-14 (NLT): *"'For I know the plans I have for you', says the Lord, 'They are plans for good and not for disaster, to give you a future and a hope. In those days when you pray, I will listen. If you look for Me wholeheartedly, you will find Me. I will be found by you,' says the Lord. 'I will end your captivity and restore your fortunes. I will gather you out of the nations where I sent you and bring you home again to your own land.'"*

So, God has plans for us which are good, not for disaster; future hope, bringing us home so that we can be at home within ourselves and find rest. We can self-medicate our anxiety, our fear of scarcity or our fear of inadequacy, with busyness. We attempt to run from the pain of life. Dallas

Willard says, *"Hurry is the enemy of our spiritual growth"*.[7] Stop! Breathe!

Walter Adams said, *"Hurry is the death of prayer and only impedes and spoils our work. It never advances it."*[8] Jesus was not in a hurry; He was present to the moment, with God, and so He could embrace interruptions: He was a non-anxious presence. Dallas Willard writes, *"I cannot live in the Kingdom of God with a hurried soul."*

I cannot rest in God with a hurried soul. John Ortberg responds, *"Guilty as charged. I quickly slip from outward busyness to inward hurriedness and my joy, peace, and clarity of purpose are the casualties."*[9]

PRAYER

Father God, Please help me to enter the place of rest – that shalom where wholeness is restored and I cease to strive.

Give me courage to lay down all the unnecessary burdens I carry. Help me to name them and give them to You.

Release me from all the false guilt I experience when, "I am not busy."

Help me to give myself permission to experience that which gives me joy and meaning.

I want to walk through the archway of trust into a place of settled security.

Amen.

Chapter 2

LEARNING TO REST IN THE SLOW LANE

Slow lane to where? The journey to rest and all that means. To begin with, we need to know that we can change. Not all cultures have always believed this and, indeed, many people ask, 'Can a leopard change its spots?' Even within the Church some doubt exists that there can be transformation, deliverance and healing for people. The ancient Greeks believed that we are what we are, and we cannot change what we are. They believed the character one was born with was one's destiny. They realised that it may take great courage to fulfil that destiny and considered that heroes were born, not made. Aristotle believed that some were born to rule, and others were born to be ruled. Anything foretold by the gods meant there was nothing anyone could do to change it. This thread of fate weaves itself through some cultures and is the complete opposite to the Bible's teaching.

In the story of Jonah there was a decree (foretelling): *In forty days Nineveh will be destroyed.* But the people of Nineveh repented, and the decree was cancelled. There is no fate that is final here, thus in complete contrast in ancient Hebrew culture there was a thread of *faith* woven through their history. Judaism appears to be the first system to develop a clear sense of human free will. That is, we can decide we are going to learn from our mistakes and act differently in future. This inspires a determination to be a changed, different person, which is good but only brings about behavioural change. God wants to change us from the inside out! However, even the idea that we can change, that we are not predestined to continue as we are, is a concept still challenged today. Some people believe our character and actions are determined by our genes, our DNA.

We cannot dismiss the nature/nurture debate. A story that illustrates this well is of an adopted neuroscientist who, as a hobby, liked jumping out of aeroplanes. His adoptive father was a neurologist and his grandfather a surgeon. His choice of career was a clear case of environment, nurture and learned expectations. However, he later met his birth father, who turned out to be an airline pilot with a love of aeroplanes: an inherited, genetic disposition!

We have a generational inheritance. We are influenced by both nature and nurture and both affect our present. There is a direct line of continuity between past and present. We didn't arrive here out of nowhere; we are influenced by our family of origin. In one of his podcasts, John Mark Comer illustrates these generational patterns through the story of Abraham's family. In Genesis 12:1-3 (MSG) God speaks a blessing over Abraham. He is to be a conduit of blessing to the world: *"Leave and I will make you a great nation and bless you. I'll make you famous and you will be a blessing. I will bless those who bless you; those who curse you I'll curse. All the families of the earth will be blessed through you."*

In Genesis 20:10, we read that Abraham settles between Kadesh and Shur. The king takes Sarah, Abraham's wife, but Abraham lies and says, "She's my sister" because he thought the king would kill him for his wife. In Genesis 26:1-10, we read that Isaac, Abraham's son, goes down between Kadesh and Shur on his way to Egypt. God appears to him and tells him to stay put. The king is the same king as when Abraham was living there. A man asks about Rebecca, Isaac's wife. "She's my sister," he answers. Same place, same king, same lie. Isaac's son, Jacob, lies to him – a next-generational pattern of lying.

Generational sin has consequences. This can be seen in families where there is alcoholism. We have expressions such as, 'Like mother, like daughter', 'Chip off the old block'. Indeed, one of the biblical words for sin means 'bending towards', 'a vulnerability'.

Our past has shaped our present, but does not have to shape our future. The current thinking is that who we are is influenced by a mixture of 50% nature and 50% nurture. We all have a family story. When we think about such sin patterns as anger, criticism, resentment, sulking or negativity, we can see we are often a combination of learned behaviour (environment or lack of nurture) and an inherited predisposition towards. Predisposition is not the same as predestination or predetermination.

We are not to use our past as an excuse, but neither are we to deny, minimize or dismiss it. We may try to 'hide behind' scripture, quoting verses like Philippians 3:13 about forgetting the past, but that would be a misuse of Paul's words. Paul, as an elite Pharisee – with its attendant status and privilege – was writing about giving up his past good works. He was making the point that it counted as nothing compared to knowing Jesus.

We will not journey with rest if we put ourselves on a self-improvement programme. Changed behaviour is not enough; we have to repent and trust the Holy Spirit to bring revelation. I repeat, God wants to change us from the inside out. Repentance means opening up and being honest about our inner world. So much of resting on our journey is about being deeply connected to God, not keeping up appearances.

GENERATIONAL PRAYER

Father God,

I come to You with my family inheritance. I ask, Lord Jesus, that Your body on the cross will come between me and previous generations.

I name (*confess any known family sin*) and ask for it to go to You on the cross.

I repent on behalf of my family and ask You will set me free from the consequences of the sin.

I pray where this has affected my genetic code you will cleanse, heal and bring to life those genes that have atrophied, and restore to me my original DNA.

I also pray I will be blessed by the good and the potential You wanted me to inherit.

Amen.

Jeremiah 17:7-8: *"But blessed is the one who trusts in the LORD, whose confidence is in him. They will be like a tree planted by the water that sends out its roots by the stream. It does not fear when heat comes; its leaves are always green. It has no worries in a year of drought and never fails to bear fruit."*

This delicious fruit is love, joy, peace, patience, kindness, goodness, faithfulness, gentleness and self-control. *"Make a tree good and its fruit will be good; or make a tree bad and its fruit will be bad, for a tree is recognised by its fruit."* (Matthew 12:33)

The fruit tells you about the tree. Simply cutting off the branches that produce bad fruit will only deal with the appearance of the tree. It will fail to eradicate the problem which is at a deeper level. This means, rather than focusing on the bad fruit, for example behaviour, we must deal with the diseased roots of past hurts, traumas, disappointments or deprivation. We have both healthy and diseased roots exactly like we have healthy and unhealthy behaviour patterns. So, let's look at some of the conditions needed; the good earth needed to grow healthy roots.[10]

1. Unconditional love

This love needs to be expressed. I knew my parents loved me because they didn't *not* love me, but the love was not expressed in a way that met my needs. Every child is different. I felt so different from my parents that I sometimes wondered if I was adopted! Discovering evidence that I wasn't felt like a disappointment because I no longer had an explanation for the fact that I felt so unknown. My Dad would tell *others* how much he loved 'his girls'. I can remember overhearing him at the tennis club proudly talking about us to his friends, but he never told *us*. His unhealed wounds from childhood left him with a covered orphaned heart and a fear of intimacy.

2. We need to feel secure and comforted

Children need to be physically safe. In some homes, for a variety of reasons, this need is not met. Addiction may lead to explosive rage and anger, which is terrifying, causing deep insecurities and hyper-vigilance. We also need to feel emotionally secure and comforted. In an atmosphere of acceptance, where the parents are secure, a child can express fears, negative emotions and even exuberant dreams. A safe, comforting, secure environment also means children are shielded from the burden of worries they can't cope with – for example, family worries beyond their control. Or parents can leave children to 'fight their own fights', out of the mistaken belief that it is good for them. This can cause great fear, often covered by a tough exterior; not a good recipe for healthy adulthood.

3. Praise and affirmation

We all need praise and affirmation. Another word for this is 'encouragement'. When it is truthful, it strengthens us. Children who are not praised and affirmed are left hungry for approval. This makes us people-pleasers, often leading to a lack of boundaries.[11] We may spend the rest of our lives trying to gain parental approval. Part of my healing was when I realised my parents were never going to give me what I needed. They were unable to speak intimate, affirming words. I was about 35 years old at the time and chose, at a deep level, to accept them as they were; to accept their limitations. Part of their withholding of praise was a fear that my sister and I would grow up big-headed, thinking too much of ourselves. In some families there is also an excess of teasing, which can be very damaging. Having to negotiate the taunts, nicknames and teasing at school is bad enough, but having to endure this at home can lead to deep wounding.

4. Purpose in life

We need to know that we are unique, that we have talents, and that God has a purpose and a plan for our lives. We need to know that we have value. Growing up in a family with an emotionally absent father, I had no sense of my identity nor of any value. Not only does God want us to have an intimate relationship with Him, whereby we know we are loved, He wants us to know why we are here, that we were created for a purpose. For many of us it is not that we have forgotten we have a purpose; we were never told we had a purpose! This causes us to feel lost and life appears meaningless.

If we realise that any of these four basic emotional needs have not been met, we need to turn to Father God for our healing. Robert Karen writes that emotionally healthy young people, who are both self-reliant and able to rely on others, had home lives in which both parents were loving and emotionally generous.[12]

Jesus came as the good shepherd and explained in John 10:10 that He came to give us life in all its fullness, overflowing. Holy Spirit came to make this a reality. For us to experience a life fully lived; an abundant life, an overflowing life, a better life than we have ever dreamed of. What does that feel like? How does it work? We need to know that we are unconditionally loved by God in the depths of our being – whatever happens we are still loved. We need to know the Father's love in such a way that we experience security, connection and belonging.

The process for this is the healing of our past wounds, with the subsequent transformation of our head and hearts. The consequence is that we are able to live in 'unforced rhythms of grace' (an easy yoke, a light burden) from which we can invite others to join us on the journey to rest. Having established that the past affects the present, we need to accept that we all travel at different speeds and all have different obstacles to overcome. However, let's have a quick overview of some of these. The goal is growth – the ability to choose life, to choose 'becoming' – and it is about internal change, not outward appearance.[13]

Healing of memories

Physiologically and psychologically, memories and actual events affect us in similar ways, so we can re-traumatise ourselves by continually remembering it, going over the past. The power of memory to make the past present to us in a very real way is extraordinary. The answer to all this is Jesus, who is outside of time and to whom all times are present. The past, present and future time sequence, in which we experience existence, comes together with the eternal. The essential difference between some therapies and the action of the Holy Spirit in the healing of memories is the Spirit's work of pointing us to the presence of Jesus, who is there. We are enabled – with the eyes of our heart – to see Jesus in the midst of the unfolding memory drama. We receive from Him that healing word, glance or embrace we've needed for so long. We forgive others their sins against us; we confess our sins and receive love and healing grace. When we forgive at this level, we are applying the forgiveness at the place it was intended, in the deep heart.

Like photographs in albums that get wet, painful, repressed memories get stuck together with tears, which is why some memories are superimposed onto others. Also, before the age of reason – around seven or eight years old – the information we are given is not challenged.

I had a cousin who was ten years older than me and her boyfriend was my idol! He was in the army and told me he was fighting in Cyprus. Every day I would listen to the one o'clock news to make sure he was safe. I was about seven and my reasoning was that if he had been injured or killed his name would be read out. My cousin married him and one day, when I was in my twenties, I remarked, "You were in Cyprus weren't you," and he started laughing. Then he jokingly said, "Yes, and I managed to come home every weekend." Even as an adult I had held these two pieces of information unchallenged.

Pre-birth

Even what happens to us in the womb is recorded and affects us. I prayed with a little boy who was eight years old and was sent to me by a psychiatrist. He had been born with a medical condition (exomphalos) whereby most of his organs were outside of his body. He had undergone a lot of surgery to have his kidney, liver and everything put back in, so he had been born very sick. The reason he was sent to me was that he was wrecking his room, ripping the pictures off the wall and clawing at the walls. His behaviour was quite easy to sort out because he saw himself as a monster and so he acted like a monster. It is not just what has happened to us that needs healing but the subsequent distorted image of ourselves, the lies we believe about ourselves need healing, so together we did some healing of the imagination.

Children like imagining games, so we imagined Jesus coming, who told him he was Superman. I said, "Jesus always tells the truth," and his behaviour improved. However, on a subsequent visit, I asked God to help me bring some further healing to him and I felt it was right to pray for him in the womb. I didn't tell him; I just said that we were going on an imagination trip and he was to swim down and go into a cave and then he was to tell me what had happened. So he did this, and when he was in the cave he said to me, "Oh, the cave is getting smaller or I am getting bigger," so I knew that God was there. Then he said, "There is an enemy black submarine coming along. I have been attacked. I have been attacked by a submarine," and he said he was wounded.

Then he saw a bright light and was pushed towards this bright light, and as he arrived in the bright light, he was taken into a chamber where it was all white with metal machines where he was tortured. This was obviously as he was born and taken away. He received much healing and comfort from the prayer. This was my first experience of pre-birth memories. God really wanted to show me, through this child, that we have pre-birth memory, because I hadn't talked to the boy about this; he couldn't have known where he was going and yet had this incredible pre-birth memory. Since then, I have prayed for people who have had an unsafe time in the womb due to previous miscarriages, abortions or the loss of a twin.

The same principles apply for anything that needs healing in our childhood. Without striving – having settled ourselves in a place of rest – we ask the Holy Spirit to bring into our conscious minds events from the past that need healing. This is not normally chronological, as it would appear that memories are stored around emotions rather than in linear time. We then ask Jesus to reveal His presence. We do not ask Him to come, as He has always been there. It is just that we were blind, unaware of Him being with us. We watch and see what He does and then forgive or confess as we feel led. We ask God to release us from the lies that the trauma has caused us to believe about ourselves, God or others. We also ask for any revelation about any curses, verbal or non-verbal, that we may have made.

A man, Colin (not his real name), came to see me because he was totally unable to cuddle and touch his wife, though he was able to have sex with her. He was also unable to cuddle or to touch the children. After a few sessions, when we had looked into all this, it became apparent that his father had been a womaniser and Colin had seen his mother hurt. As he came into teenage life (the parents already having divorced) he was introduced to several of his father's girlfriends. However, at around the age of nine or ten, when the divorce had been going through, he had made a vow to himself, "I will never ever be like my father."

The way that was manifesting was that he disapproved of any preliminary flirtations with the opposite sex, including touching. He was totally 'paralysed'. He had to confess the words of the vow he had made and renounce them. I then prayed that these curse words would be absorbed by Jesus who, on the cross, became a curse for our sakes (Galatians 3:13).

PRAYER

Father God,

I am beginning to recognise the family I grew up in did not provide the good earth I needed to grow and flourish.

I lift to You the lack of unconditional love (*allow the Holy Spirit to bring to mind memories. Confess any internal decisions you made, lies about yourself you believed, forgive everyone and everything and then ask for the Father's healing words*).

I bring to You the memories where I did not feel safe (*use the same process as before*).

I bring to You the lack of affirmation and ask You to heal me from all the negative words my family spoke over me (*Now wait for the Father's encouraging words*).

And Father, please heal me from all the meaninglessness and lack of purpose I experienced and let me know in my deepest inner being that You have a plan for my life.

Amen.

Understanding how traumas in our lives cause diseased roots is one issue, but lack of nurturing can equally affect us, sometimes even more deeply. Emotional neglect or deprivation is difficult to recognise but the effects leave us emotionally malnourished.

Emotional deprivation/neglect

When we hear that God loves us, we usually have a level of agreement about the statement, but for some of us it is interpreted by our heart as a distant, slightly disinterested concern for our welfare and wellbeing.

Really loves us?
Yes – He is not someone a bit old, benevolently wanting us to be happy in our own way.
Really loves us?
Yes – He is not a judge making sure we obey the law for our own sake.
Really loves us?
Yes – Julian of Norwich writes, "We have always been loved. There has never been a time when we have not been loved."

In Biblical times, the shepherd was a warrior as well as a gentle caregiver, both protecting and nurturing. God really loves us! His is a passionate, consuming love, a persistent, creative love, a jealous love, a love so great it is beyond our comprehension and, but for moments of grace, beyond our desiring. Why is that? Well, I believe this is partly linked to deprivation and neglect. Before some of you immediately decide that is not you, let me give a few pointers.

You will have been deprived if your parents were not Christians, because you would have not been nurtured as a child of the covenant; you have no deeply taught understanding of your inheritance or destiny. This was true for me, so I was unable to rest, as I was forever striving to fulfil my self-imposed improvement programme.

You will have been deprived if one or both of your parents were emotionally absent; there was no deep intimacy, for whatever reason. You will have been deprived if your interests, education or hobbies were different from your family and you felt lonely, isolated and were never encouraged in what you wanted to pursue. My sister and parents were very sociable and couldn't understand why I didn't want to go out and play. I also had a good imagination, which no-one understood, and when I was an adult my mother once commented, "You always were a funny little thing!"

Emotional deprivation is what occurs when we have been emotionally neglected, overlooked or never encouraged to join in, maybe because everyone was too busy or overworked or there was a problem person around whom the family revolved. Maybe we came from a family that 'didn't do emotions', where we didn't express intimacy or where we felt our problems or needs would be the final straw, would rock the boat too much. This is particularly true for a child who perceives either parent to be overloaded or emotionally fragile. I felt my mother was a fragile princess because this was how my father treated her. This was an internalised feeling.

Or we can come from a family where emotional struggles are seen as weakness and are shaming. Emotional neglect is when our parents do not respond enough to our emotions in childhood or help us to contain them. It is when we aren't noticed, validated or when emotions aren't talked about. As a child, we then learn that emotions are useless, troublesome or shameful – something to be denied – and so detach from them. This results in a deep emptiness and a 'disconnect' from part of ourselves. We experience countless times of superficial conversations or discussions without action or solution. I realised later in life that many times I would want to leave family occasions because I felt the true me was being overlooked, seemingly invisible to everyone else. Only certain aspects of me were acknowledged. This left me feeling bored and saddened, even though nothing hurtful had happened.

Another form of emotional neglect is where there is an 'enmeshment' with one or other of the parents. This form of confused love does not allow the child its separate existence. The child's identity, views and emotional needs are swallowed up in such a way that the child is part of the parent. There are no boundaries between parent and child. I had one young man who, on telling his story, said, "And when I was eight years old, we got divorced." When I enquired who got divorced, he replied, "Mother and I divorced him." Another young man declared, "My mother is so spiritually attuned to me that she always rings when I am a bit down and struggling." I asked if he thought we should pray and ask Jesus to stand between them. He wasn't sure, saying, "What will happen to mother?"

On another occasion a young woman said to her mother, "I will have to die when you die", to which the mother answered, "Then I will have to keep well!" In all these examples there is no separation, no containment and no allowance made for the truth that the child can exist on their own.

With this type of neglect, we end up overly dependent on the parent and unable to grow up. Or we develop a form of 'defensive detachment'. We become an observer, always feeling slightly on the outside and very often not really minding. This detachment can make us cynical: "It's okay for them, but it never happens for me." Annoyed by others' emotions, yet so defensive, we are unable to get in touch with our own heart needs. A more generous statement, but still detached, is "As long as they are happy, I am".

Defensive detachment towards God may be hidden with thoughts such as: "I fear being overwhelmed; I am afraid of my own emotions, I fear my emotions will betray me or let me down, as in the past. I need to stay in control. If I give myself permission to express my emotions, I don't know where it will stop. If I start crying or shouting, I may never stop."

Or this kind of deprivation can make us very emotionally 'hungry', dependent and always needing more. Proverbs 27:7 (NLT) says, *"Honey seems tasteless to the person who is full, but even bitter food tastes sweet to the hungry."* It is a feeling of scarcity – not enough of anything.

Lynne Twist writes: *"For me, and for many of us, our first waking thought of the day is, 'I didn't get enough sleep.' The next one is, 'I don't have enough time.' Whether true or not, the thought of 'not enough' occurs to us automatically before we even think to question or examine it. We spend most of the hour and the days of our lives hearing, explaining, complaining or worrying about what we don't have enough of ... we don't have enough exercise; we don't have enough work; we don't have enough profits; we don't have enough power; we don't have enough weekends; or, of course, we don't have enough money – ever. Before we even sit up in bed, before our feet touch the floor, we're already inadequate, already behind, already losing, already lacking something. And by the time we go to bed at night our minds race with a litany of what we didn't get or didn't get done that day. We go to sleep burdened by those thoughts and wake up to lack. What begins as a simple expression of the hurried life, or even the challenged life, grows into the great justification for an unfulfilled life."*[14]

And what little we have, we must hang on to. The friend is not enough – ever – may even be toxic – but better than nothing.

In Exodus 16, Moses tells the people to gather as much manna as they needed, about two quarts per person. Those who gathered much, when it was measured, had no extra, and those who gathered less weren't short. Each had enough. Moses had said, "Don't leave any until morning," but some did, and it went mouldy and smelled bad. Hanging on to stuff that is toxic doesn't work. We need to trust God that he will provide enough. But we also need to know we are allowed to receive the provision.

Emotional neglect can be caused because our parents have never felt eligible to join us in the lifestyle they provided for us. My father was a successful businessman with an orphaned heart. Despite, probably, having more money than the other dads in my class, my father never felt eligible, didn't feel 'as good as'. This poem expresses it well.

The Railings by Roger McGough

You came to watch me playing cricket once.
Quite a few of the fathers did,
At ease, outside the pavilion.
They would while away a Sunday afternoon,
Joke with the masters, urge on
Their flannelled offspring.
But not you.
Fielding deep near the boundary

29

I saw you through the railings.
You were embarrassed when I waved
And moved out of sight down the road.
When it was my turn to bowl though
I knew you'd still be watching.
Third ball, a wicket, and three more followed.
When we came in at the end of the innings
The other Dads applauded and joined us for tea.
Of course you'd gone by then. Later,
You said you'd found yourself there by accident,
Just passing. Spotted me through the railings.
Speech days. Prize-givings. School plays.
The twenty-first. The wedding. The Christening.
You would find yourself there by accident.
Just passing.
Spotted me through the railings.

PRAYER

Father God,

You are the source of all being. Come, I ask, and bless me with Your love and comfort in all the under-nourished, empty areas of my life.

I thank You that You are the God that sees. Help me to know and experience this in the places where I have been overlooked, not been given attention, and not listened to.

Amen.

In order to continue our journey, we need to acknowledge how our traumas have shaped us and, with patience towards ourselves, seek healing. As part of this, we need to know how to own our feelings, recognising when our reactions are 'over the top'. Usually when this happens, we have to ask the Holy Spirit to help us see why the present moment has caused more of an impact because of a past event. Even after we have received significant healing, there may be 'bruising 'or 'tenderness' around the original wound. We need to learn to exercise gentleness towards ourselves.

It is a legitimate expectation to be seen and not to be treated as invisible. Since emotions are a personal expression of who we are, if our parents have been unable to acknowledge our emotions, then we believe the lie that we are not worth seeing. We need to repent of this. We also need to stop playing games, for example sitting quietly waiting to see if anyone notices us or remembers something we told them. When I was less healed than I am now, on returning from holiday, instead of mentioning something about my experience, I would play the waiting game to see if anyone remembered I had been on holiday, checking to see if anyone was interested in me!

As I have written before, our feelings need to be listened to, nurtured and educated. Listening to our feelings means we 'sit with them'. We do not avoid them by detaching from them or by getting busy. We nurture them by acknowledging that we have a feeling and that it is permissible to be experiencing these emotions. We ask Jesus to sit with us and help us understand them. We educate our feelings by asking the Holy Spirit to help us make the connection between the past and the present. We reassure our feelings in such a way that we are not overwhelmed by them. A fear of abandonment will not cause us to act in unhealthy ways because we can acknowledge the feeling, it is very powerful, but we can allow ourselves to feel the feeling without acting out, whilst speaking truth to ourselves, such as 'I am not powerless' or 'Jesus is with me'.

When we have not been taught well to understand our emotions, we can be slow reactors. I am. It will take me a few days to recognise something has upset me or that I am hurt. Often people will tell me they feel a bit down, but they don't know why. We have to ask the Holy Spirit to take us back over the last few days to where the incident took place and bring revelation.

In educating our emotions, we need to name them. A few months after my husband died, I found myself looking at the clock one late afternoon and, seeing it was five o'clock, thought, "Five hours before I can go to bed." I then experienced a dreadful feeling. I asked Jesus what it was. 'Anxious loneliness' was the reply. I resisted the temptation of avoiding the feeling by getting busy or tidying a cupboard in restless activity and decided to stay with Jesus and the feeling. It took well over an hour to subside. I have experienced it on three other occasions, each time shorter and with less severity.

So, what do we leave behind if we are going to experience rest on the journey? What does letting go entail? We let go of going over past bad news, past injustices against us or our own past failures and ask for a new way of thinking. Larry Harp expresses this well in the following story:

Leaving the City of Regret

"I had not really planned on taking a trip this time of year, and yet I found myself packing rather hurriedly. This trip was going to be unpleasant, and I knew in advance that no real good would come out of it. I'm talking about my annual 'guilt trip'. I got tickets to fly there on *Wish I Had* airlines. It was an extremely short flight. I got my baggage, which I could not check. I chose to carry it myself all the way. It was weighed down with a thousand memories of what might have been. No-one greeted me as I entered the terminal to the *Regret City International Airport.* I say 'international' because people from all over the world come to this dismal town.

"As I checked into *The Last Resort Hotel* I noticed that they would be hosting the year's most important event, *The Annual Pity Party.* I wasn't going to miss that great social occasion. Many of the town's leading citizens would be there. First, there would be the *Done* family, you know, *Should Have, Would Have* and *Could Have.* Then came the *I Had* family. You probably know ol' *Wish* and his clan. Of course, the *Opportunities* would be present, *Missed* and *Lost.* The biggest family would be the *Yesterdays.* There are far too many of them to count but each one would have a very sad story to share. Then *Shattered Dreams* would surely make an appearance and *It's Their Fault* would regale us with stories (excuses) about how things had failed in his life, and each story would be loudly applauded by *Don't Blame Me* and *I Couldn't Help It.*

"Well, to make a long story short, I went to this depressing party knowing that there would be no real benefit in doing so. And, as usual, I became very depressed. But as I thought about all the stories of failures brought back from the past, it occurred to me that all of this trip and subsequent 'pity party' could be cancelled by ME! I started to truly realise that I did not have to be there! I didn't have to be depressed. One thing kept going through my mind, 'I CAN'T

CHANGE YESTERDAY BUT I DO HAVE THE POWER TO MAKE TODAY A WONDERFUL DAY!' I can be happy, joyous, fulfilled, encouraged, as well as encouraging. Knowing this, I left The City of Regret immediately and left no forwarding address. Am I sorry for mistakes I've made in the past? YES! But there is no physical way to undo them."

We need to let go of old scripts. This first came to me in a dream about five years ago. In the dream I was sitting with a group of people learning my part of a script. I asked Jesus to come and help me. Jesus said, 'I can, or you can join me with My script, but you have to let go of *your* script.' I awoke, not with excitement but with some trepidation and fear. What did it mean? But I trusted and said yes. Over the next week I had a couple more dreams explicitly speaking of certain issues which led to a radical reshaping of The Healing Prayer School ministry.

Jesus goes before us and creates a place where He invites us to join Him. Ephesians 2:10 in The Message reads, *"It's God's gift from start to finish! We don't play the major role. If we did, we'd probably go around bragging that we'd done the whole thing! No, we neither make nor save ourselves. God does both the making and saving. He creates each of us by Christ Jesus to join him in the work he does, the good work he has gotten ready for us to do, work we had better be doing."*

We were created for good works, but not any good works; the works God has created uniquely for each of us. C S Lewis writes, *"The Christian is in a different position from other people who are trying to be good. They hope, by being good, to please God if there is one; or – if they think there is not – at least they hope to deserve approval from good men.*

But the Christian thinks any good he does comes from the Christ-life inside him. He does not think God will love us because we are good, but that God will make us good because He loves us"[15]

In his book, "Jesus is Better Than You Imagined", Jonathan Merritt has some interesting insights into scripts. The following is an adaptation of his thoughts.

Thesis 1: Everybody lives by a script
The script may be implicit or explicit. It may be recognised or unrecognised, but everybody has a script.

Thesis 2: We get scripted
All of us get scripted through the process of nurture and formation and socialization, and it happens to us without our knowing it.

Thesis 3: You have a family script
My personal script was, 'by working hard and playing hard you will be self-made and have a successful life.'

Thesis 4: The script promises to make us safe and happy
Enacted through advertising, propaganda and ideology, especially television.

Thesis 5: That script has failed
It cannot make us safe, and it cannot make us happy.

We are constantly scripted by the liturgies of our culture. We are given a story that is meant to shape our lives and our imaginations, and for the most part we are completely unaware that this is happening. We need to let go and disengage from the script. However, most of us, if we are honest, feel profoundly ambivalent about this because we like parts of it and resist completely moving away from it. We need to be 'de-scripted' and truly know, *"Unless the Lord builds the house, those that build it labour in vain"* (Psalm 127:1 ESVUK). Our task is to continually articulate the alternative script rooted in the Bible.

Script 1: Let go of an achievement-based identity.

We build our identity on gaining things or achieving in the world. Jesus, in essence, says, "To follow me you have to take up your cross." We have to lose our life in order to gain/save our life. The word here for 'life' in Greek is 'psyche', from which we get the world psychology. It's our identity, personality, our being – that which makes us unique. Jesus is not saying, "I want you to lose your individual self." What He is saying is, "Don't build your identity on gaining things – status, goods, education – that which the world judges as of value and superior." Most family or culture scripts will be based on performance and achievement. Jesus is saying, "I don't want you to move from one performance-based script to another. I want your identity to be in your relationship with Me."

Script 2: Let go of trying to find ourselves.

Our real self will not come while we are looking for it. It will be slowly revealed to us when we are looking at Jesus. C S Lewis writes: *"The more we get what we call 'ourselves' out of the way and let Him take us over, the more truly ourselves we become … The more I resist Him and try to live on my own, the more I become dominated by my own heredity and upbringing and surrounding and natural desires. In fact what I so proudly call 'Myself' becomes merely the meeting place for trains of events which I never started and I cannot stop. What I call 'My wishes' become merely the desires*

36

thrown up by my physical organism or pumped into me by other men's thoughts ... It is when I turn to Christ, when I give myself up to His personality, that I finally begin to have a real personality of my own ... [Nevertheless], you must not go to Christ for the sake of 'a new self'. As long as your own personality is what you are bothering about you are not going to Him at all."[16]

Jesus is creating a new kind of human being, a fresh start for everybody. Ephesians 2:14, 15 (MSG): *"The Messiah has made things up between us so that we're now together on this, both non-Jewish outsiders and Jewish insiders. He tore down the wall we used to keep each other at a distance. He repealed the law code that had become so clogged with fine print and footnotes that it hindered more than it helped. Then he started over. Instead of continuing with two groups of people separated by centuries of animosity and suspicion, he created a new kind of human being, a fresh start for everybody."*

Script 3: Let go of the law-code. Pick up the script of grace.

Jesus offers real rest, including rest from duty and religious activity. *"I suspect you would never intend this, but this is what happens. When you attempt to live by your own religious plans and projects, you are cut off from Christ, you fall out of grace. Meanwhile we expectantly wait for a satisfying relationship with the Spirit. For in Christ, neither our most conscientious religion nor disregard of religion amounts to anything. What matters is something far more interior: faith expressed in love."* Galatians 5:4-6 (MSG).

How many of you feel like this? The law leaves us empty, exhausted and burned out.

Matthew 11:28-30 (MSG):*"Are you tired? Worn out? Burned out on religion? Come to me. Get away with me and you'll recover your life. I'll show you how to take a real rest. Walk with me and work with me – watch how I do it. Learn the unforced rhythms of grace. I won't lay anything heavy or ill-fitting on you. Keep company with me and you'll learn to live freely and lightly."*

Again quoting Jonathan Merritt from his book, "Jesus is Better Than You Imagined", he speaks on how he became burned out from being a pastor of a large church.

"With the worship centre lights dimmed and only a few remaining voices echoing in from the foyer, I sat down to contemplate the impasse I'd reached. I couldn't give up on God, and yet I didn't want to continue my current spiritual path. This would mean embracing an unbearable future, one where I engaged God out of duty. We'd become an old married couple, sitting on the couch with each other each evening, rarely speaking. Sure, we'd stay together, but I'd always wonder if I'd hung around longer than I should. God, I want to stay with you, but I can't keep doing this." He goes on to write, *"Suddenly my eyes withered – my duty had blinded me to the presence of Jesus. Too busy to look and see."*

When we have this wrong view of God – when we have this 'law' view of God – like the elder son had in the story of the prodigal son, we exclude ourselves from the feast because we do not know that 'everything the Father has is ours'. We do not understand our adoption, the gospel of reconciliation or God's love, which enables us to turn to repent. Instead, we stand trying to get it right, to stay in control and trying to obey. Even obedience can be law. Sometimes you hear people saying, "God has blessed you because you were obedient". Possibly true. However, the minute we start being obedient in order to receive a blessing, we have missed it. Trying to be obedient whilst harbouring resentment, anger and bitterness in our hearts blinds us to the blessings, as it did with the elder son. Obedience – because I want to please God and deeply know His way for my life – is best and enables us to see the blessings. Grace-filled people are grateful people.

So what does a grace-filled life look like? The following story was told by Anne Coles one year during week two of the New Wine event held annually every summer. The background is that, on the large showground site, all the fields are divided into differently coloured zones such as 'Pink 1' or 'Brown 2' and individual churches are allotted a place within a zone. This particular year a lady arrived and put up her tent, only to find she was in the wrong field with the wrong church! However, the village hosts – instead of insisting she move on to make sure they were obeying the guidelines – extended grace and said she could stay if she liked, which she did. The next morning she woke up to discover that her tent was next to that of her sister, whom she had lost touch with years ago. The grace script of the village hosts made space for a God encounter!

The book of 2 Samuel contains the story of Mephibosheth, who was five years old when news came that Saul and Jonathan were both dead. His nurse – in her haste to run away – picked him and up and dropped him, causing him to become crippled in both feet. He was Jonathan's son and the presumed heir to the throne, had David not been victorious. Therefore, if David had been intent on slaughtering all the previous royal family, this little chap would have been top of the list. Moving forward twenty years, David, the shepherd king, is now successful and at peace. And maybe, reflecting on how Jonathan had saved his life and how he, in return, had promised to be kind to Jonathan's family, he asks his servant if anyone is left of Saul's family (2 Samuel 9:1). He is told that there is a crippled son living in Lo-debar (meaning 'no pasture' or 'barren place'). David invites him to the palace despite the stigma of him being crippled. Mephibosheth is anxious on arrival. He shuffles, stammers and does not look David in the eye. David tells him he is returning all the properties of his grandfather, Saul, to him, and says, "Furthermore, you will eat at my table". Mephibosheth says, "Who am I that you pay attention to a stray dog like me?" A few verses later it says, "... and Mephibosheth ate at David's table just like one of the royal family." Love and grace.

Script 4: Let go of how things should be.

I had a friend who put many of her precious possessions in storage when she had to move to a less desirable area following her divorce. For many years she nursed the lie, 'My life shouldn't be like this. This isn't what I signed up for' script. She kept her possessions in storage, waiting to move, 'life on hold'. After some healing prayer she began to accept her situation and collected her goods. Amongst them was her guitar which she loved to play and used to sing worship songs. Her resistance to accepting her life as it was had also deprived her of something she loved. She had lived with this self-imposed deprivation for about ten years. Having accepted the situation, within another two years she had managed to move to an area she loved.

Script 5: Let go of 'I want it now!'

Endurance and active perseverance are not 'I want it now' words. Hebrews 12: 1-2 (AMP): *"Therefore, since we are surrounded by so great a cloud of witnesses, [who by faith have testified to the truth of God's absolute faithfulness] stripping off every unnecessary weight and the sin which so easily and cleverly entangles us, let us run with endurance and active perseverance the race that is set before us, looking away from all that will distract us and focusing our eyes on Jesus, who is the Author and Perfecter of faith."*

The following is adapted from a *Pastoral Care Ministries* article:

"I recently scanned the New York Times' list of best-selling advice books and noticed a strong theme: results now. It's in our nature to want quick rewards for our efforts and swift gratification of our desires. Top-selling books offer a lifestyle makeover for health and weight loss in just 30 days, and decluttering that will magically transform your home in an instant. We are creatures who feel soothed and excited by the prospect of getting what we want right away. But those who have heard the call to maturity in Christ must lift their eyes to a more thrilling horizon than 'I want it now'. We are called to become the men and women we truly are who will live forever with our God, and we are called to help one another along in this becoming. We call this 'discipleship'. A publisher might have had a hard time selling many copies of a book with bright callouts on the cover that promise: **'Slow results! Imperceptible gains! You'll see change years later!'** *Yet wisdom points to the special worth of things that take time to grow, and surely our natural admiration of long-term endeavours is a gift from God."*

Ecclesiastes 3:11: *"He has made everything beautiful in its time. He has also set eternity in the human heart yet no one can fathom what God has done from beginning to end."*

God loves us enough to not want us to settle for the immediate or for second best and, as we have seen, although this is not new (think of Esau selling his birthright for a bowl of soup), our modern culture has blinded us to the value of a 'long obedience in the same direction' (Friedrich Nietzsche quote used by Eugene H Peterson as a book title). Gore Vidal has observed 'today's passion for the immediate and the casual.'

We are called to a life of purpose far beyond what we think ourselves capable of living; God can give us everything we need to fulfil our destiny. It's not always easy pursuing the Kingdom of God in a culture devoted to the Kingdom of Self, since, as well as letting go of instant gratification, we need to let go of the idea of developing power to make things happen and of cultivating image to appear important.

There are no shortcuts to growing up. The path to maturity is long and arduous. Hurry is no virtue. There is no secret 'quick fix' that can make it easier. Those recovering from addiction learn the value of committing to slow results. Patrick Carnes explains, "The process takes ultimately three to five years before cravings cease to be a day-to-day problem."[17]

When people who have embarked on a healing prayer journey with me ask, "How long?" I have two answers. The first is that the disciples spent three years in daily company with Jesus and did not appear to have everything sorted. Secondly, we have experienced x number of years of pain, trauma, being sinned against and our sinful responses, so what is three years when this offers us hope of lasting recovery and freedom from lies, a new beginning?!

Choices that cultivate perseverance are made moment by moment giving slow results and imperceptible gains but causing us to live a joyful and glorious life beyond our imagination! The sin of acedia opposes perseverance. I have written more about acedia in "Father Matters" but I want to highlight here how it hijacks perseverance and rest. The word comes from the Greek 'without care'. In essence, acedia is a slothful sadness that rejects the reality that we are here to become all that God has called us to be. We often cover this pain with overwork and busyness.

Busyness – or restless activity – is not the same as perseverance. We can use an inconsequential busyness as an avoidance mechanism. Think about a teenager who needs to do some revising but is busy sending texts and Instagrams or checking football results, busy arranging the weekend or busy helping others, especially if some drama is involved. Sometimes we avoid the race set before us – the following of Jesus – by busyness and senseless overwork because we are covering up disappointment, sorrow, emotional pain or despondency. We give up on what we should be doing and cover this up with other activities. This is acedia. Because we are outwardly busy, we deceive ourselves and others that we are persevering but in fact it is avoidance. Josef Pieper writes, *"One who is trapped in acedia has neither the courage nor the will to be as great as he really is."*[18] Usually the temptation begins after we have been journeying for a while. 'What do I have to show for all this effort?' we think. 'Is it working?' 'There must be an easier way', 'Is it really worth it?' We become more distracted, restless and dissatisfied.

Thomas Aquinas links acedia to a sin against the third commandment: *"… but the seventh day is a Sabbath for the Lord your God, on it you shall not do any work"* (Exodus

20:10). True Sabbath is only experienced by yielding to God's ways. Acedia grants no rest. Rather than yielding to God and His promised rest, in bondage to acedia we spend our efforts on a struggle *'to break out of the peace at the centre of his own being'*,[19] writes Pieper. Perseverance enables us to rest our spirit in God. The following story illustrates perseverance.

The legend of Cliff Young

Every year Australia hosts a 543.7 mile endurance race from Sydney to Melbourne. It is considered among the world's most gruelling ultra-marathons. The race takes five days to complete and is normally only attempted by world-class athletes who train specially for the event. These athletes are typically less than thirty years old and backed by large companies such as Nike.

In 1983 a man named Cliff Young showed up at the start of this race. Cliff was 61 years old and wore overalls and work boots. To everyone's shock, Cliff wasn't a spectator. He picked up his race number and joined the other runners. The press and other athletes became curious and questioned Cliff. They told him, "You're crazy, there's no way you can finish this race." To which he replied, "Yes, I can. See, I grew up on a farm where we couldn't afford horses or tractors and the whole time I was growing up, whenever the storms would roll in I'd have to go out and round up sheep. We had 2,000 sheep on 2,000 acres. Sometimes I would have to run those sheep for two or three days. It took a long time, but I'd always catch them. I believe I can run this race."

When the race started the pros quickly left Cliff behind. The crowds and television audiences were entertained because

Cliff didn't even run properly; he appeared to shuffle. Many even feared for the old farmer's safety. All the professional athletes knew that it took about five days to finish the race. In order to compete, one had to run about eighteen hours a day and sleep the remaining six hours. The thing is, Cliff Young didn't know that! When the morning of the second day came everyone was in for another surprise. Not only was Cliff still in the race but he had continued jogging all night and was in the lead (though I think they overtook him again during the day). Eventually Cliff was asked about his tactics for the rest of the race. To everyone's disbelief, he claimed he would run straight through to the finish without sleeping.

Cliff kept running. Each night he came a little closer to the leading pack. By the final night he had surpassed all the young, world-class athletes. He was the first competitor to cross the finish line and set a new course record. He was ahead by ten hours! When Cliff was awarded the winning prize of $10,000, he said he didn't know there was a prize and insisted that he did not enter for the money. He ended up giving all his winnings to the other runners, an act that endeared him to all of Australia. Apparently, the 'Young shuffle' is now adopted by many ultra-marathon runners as it is considered more evenly efficient.

We need to let go of old scripts of an achievement-based identity, trying to find ourselves, letting go of a law code, 'how things should be' and 'I want it now' and find new scripts. All of which involve patience and compassion towards ourselves as we learn to rest as we wait.

PRAYER

Father,

We know that unless we can trust You, believing You have the very best for us — more than we have ever imagined — we will not be able to let go of our scripts.

We ask for courage to let go of our way of doing things and trust You for our script.

Amen.

Rest as we wait

C S Lewis writes, *"I am sure God keeps no-one waiting unless He sees that it is good for him to wait."*[20] Our world has increased in pace in almost all aspects of our lives. Technology has changed everything. In recent history, communication of matters of importance was done by letter and one would often have to wait for an answer — no emails, texts or apps daily demanding an instant answer. Our ability to now transport vegetables and fruit around the world means we are no longer limited to eating just seasonal fruit and vegetables. Here in the UK, we can have strawberries at Christmas time; we do not have to wait for them to grow!

This is not wrong in itself, but we need to know that this physical reality has shaped our spirituality. We want God to answer as soon as we have prayed. If, as we have been seeing, we suffer from emotional neglect, we can easily allow our unhealed emotions to project onto God that this waiting is evidence that we have been overlooked, not heard or even abandoned. Learning to not be defined by these feelings helps us to be healed, trusting that whilst we are waiting, God is working.

Moreover, because of the influence of modern life, we can easily believe the lie that waiting is a waste – a waste of time and a waste of energy – because we could be getting on with things. We certainly do waste energy if we do not have a Biblical view of waiting. Jonathan Merritt illustrates this well:

The story of Noah

"When he was young, he sat around the campfire with his father Lamech and his 369-year-old great-granddaddy, Methuselah. As firelight danced off their cheekbones, Noah would listen to them tell old family stories, but his favourite was the one about great-great-grandpa Enoch. Legend had it that Enoch was so righteous and favoured by God that the Almighty finally seized him from the earth. 'I want to walk with God like Enoch did,' Noah would say to himself. And one day he would get his chance, but not before waiting 480 years. We don't know much about how Noah spent those five centuries except that, like his ancestor Enoch, "He found favour in the eyes of the Lord … Noah was a righteous man, blameless among the people of his time and he walked with God". For Noah, waiting on the Lord was an opportunity to walk with the Lord.

"When he was almost half a millennium old, God came to him with some mixed news. The world had gone to pot and the wickedness of humans was so great that God regretted creating them. He decided to wipe the slate clean and start over. But Noah would be spared, God said, if he performed one simple task: build a boat. I suspect Noah thought back to Enoch in that moment because he didn't flinch an inch at

God's request to construct an ark half the size of the Titanic. He just started building.

"The Bible says that the first pitter-patter of rain was heard when Noah was six hundred years old. God waited 120 years after his instructions to Noah, but scholars believe the construction project took a maximum of about seventy-five years. Why make Noah wait an extra forty-five years? Why allow him to endure the sneers and jeers of all the doubters and haters? Why not flood the earth the moment the last nail was driven into the last plank? (Spurgeon writes that maybe he was waiting for the tortoise to arrive!).

"Once the storm begins God makes him wait again, this time for forty days and nights inside the cramped vessel until the rain stops pouring. He almost loses his mind as he rushes around, feeding, cleaning, muttering prayers. A few days in he starts to feel claustrophobic but he stays beneath the deck to avoid the sight and stench of waterlogged animals floating by. After a month and a half of seasickness and clinging to God like a life-preserver, Noah finds dry land and emerges from the watery wasteland. God promises never to send another flood like that again. He offers a rainbow as a reminder and says that He will remember His words every time He sees it, and Noah trusts that God will always look in the right direction.

Though the tale of Noah's flood is often romanticised, it is no childhood fable. Noah faced an event so mentally and emotionally traumatic that the world's best counsellor would be of no use. Why did God make Noah wait another forty-five years before sending rain?"[21]

Other characters in the Bible experienced waiting:

- God made Abraham and Sarah wait nearly one hundred years before the promised son was born.
- Joseph had to wait for years as a slave and prisoner before God promoted him to Pharaoh's palace and allowed him to face his backstabbing brothers.
- For forty years Moses waited in the desert before God called him to rescue the Israelites.
- After David was anointed king, God made him wait more than a decade to assume the throne.
- Paul, after his conversion, had to wait to start his ministry.

The Psalmist sang (Psalm 62:1), *"My soul waits in silence for God."* In Isaiah 40:31, Isaiah writes, *"Those that wait on the Lord shall renew their strength."* James 1:1-12 is all about enduring, buffeting and waiting. God's people waited four hundred years after the last book of the Old Testament was penned before He came. Once here, He makes them wait another thirty years before He begins His ministry. After the crucifixion, Jesus makes the disciples wait three days for the resurrection. After all, the disciples were soaking in grief and confusion during that time. And once Jesus returns to them He promises to send the Holy Spirit. But not immediately. "Do not leave Jerusalem," Jesus tells them, "but wait for the gift my Father promised."

It is not a case of, 'Will we have to wait?' but, 'Will we learn to wait well... wait for the good fruit to grow?'

And in our journey of rest, we need to learn to take small steps.

Small risks every day

Gerald Sittser writes, "I doubt that any of the missionaries and martyrs of the past had any idea what would eventually become of their lives when they first began to entertain the thought of mission work. The work to which they gave themselves unfolded over a long period of time. Each decision, event, experience and sacrifice, which might have seemed small and insignificant at the time, prepared them for the next. The cumulative effect was great indeed, though I am not sure that it seemed that way when they were in the middle of it. Perhaps that is the point. We read a brief synopsis of their stories, viewing the whole as if it were a landscape painting. We see the entirety of their lives in a single moment – Jim Elliot murdered by Indians becoming an American martyr, Studd's journey from British athlete to African evangelist, Slessor's journey from factory girl to tribal mediator, Carey's journey from a poor cobbler to a translator and professor. But they lived the story, day after day, year after year, not knowing how it would all turn out. Their work progressed slowly and unpredictably and mysteriously. They made little decisions every day to do the will of God as they knew it; they took little risks – as well as a few big ones – that set them on a course leading to adventure, achievement and influence; they chose to devote their time, talent and energy to God, refusing to put limits on what God would do with them."[22]

The enemy loves to tempt us with a technicolour, dramatic, adventurous version of what living life to the full really means. He attempted this with Jesus in Matthew 4:8 when Satan gestures expansively at all the earth's kingdoms, showing how glorious they are and saying to Jesus, in essence, "Worship me and they are yours". Unfortunately, Satan has more success with us than he did with Jesus. We are often tempted to listen to the devil's grandiosity, hungry for the 'prophetic' word that will promise us fame and influence. The danger is that this deafens us to the 'lullaby' of Jesus who wants to love us and have us follow Him in our garden, kitchen or workplace, for example. So we need to learn to live in the reality of today, not in any fantasy or parallel life whereby we are always waiting to become 'someone' or someone else or be somewhere else, but in today where Christ dwells. Living today means we do not put life on hold until everything is sorted out or until we 'get there', the 'somewhere over the rainbow'. Life is now.

When I became a Christian, if God had said to me, "You will take a group of people all round the world teaching and ministering healing prayer, you will preach in a cathedral and write several books," I would have been left wondering which one of us was mad! It was all small steps. As I have written elsewhere, it all began with a small group of a few mums wanting to learn to hear God. At the time, the Church I belonged to (and still do) was a gospel believing evangelical church with little to no experience of signs and wonders. I had been filled with the Spirit in a small church about five miles away. There was a very loving, thriving Young Wives group who really loved and looked after one another. Anyone who had a baby was quickly visited with a home-made cake. Ellie, my longstanding prayer partner, and I had the thought that when we took a cake, which we would do together, we would also offer to pray for the new mum – there and then, out loud. A radical, small step, a small risk, but it was a beginning. It never occurred to us at the time that it would lead to words of knowledge and prayers for healing. We just took the first step.

So let us begin where I began, learning to listen to God.

Chapter 3

A LISTENING HEART

St Augustine of Hippo said, *"Thou has made us for Thyself, O Lord, and our heart is restless until it finds its rest in You."* Even after we have found God, often we remain restless. Why is this? We become content with far less than God has for us. What does spiritual maturity look like to you? How often do we experience extravagant worship whereby we sing, dance and demonstrate our love? When were you last accused of being drunk, not on wine but on the Holy Spirit?!

Whenever we judge someone else's freedom, we put to death some of our childlike capacity to worship without being self-conscious, without awareness of others around us. We self-censor our ability to be filled with wonder and fully present to Jesus. We may thereby approach God with obligation and maybe, even, with boredom. This restlessness or, if we are brave enough to acknowledge it, our dissatisfaction, can be a mixture of church culture and how we think we should behave as Christians.

God made us to worship. Worship in Psalm 47 appears quite emotional and noisy. There is clapping, there are cries and shouts of joy, trumpets and lots of singing! We are good at expressing our emotions in other contexts, such as at football matches, or at pop festivals, and often we leave with a satisfied heart, having experienced the freedom of expressing ourselves. But if we have a distorted view of God in our heart, we will not want to worship Him. So we need to explore what God is like.

A six-year-old was drawing a picture one day. Her teacher asked, "What are you drawing?" The little girl answered, "I am drawing a picture of God." The teacher was surprised and said, "But nobody knows what God looks like?!" The little girl carried on drawing and replied, "They will in a minute."[23]

The German preacher, Meister Eckhart, expressed himself very strongly in the cry of his heart, "God! Deliver me from God!" What he was referring to was the shadowy concept/perception of God. Eckhart had created and worshipped an image of God, not God Himself. Someone said, 'God made man in His own image and we have returned the compliment'. I had a teenage boy visit one morning in a great panic. "I don't believe in God any more," he blurted out. "It's alright," I replied, "The sun is still going to rise and is still going to set, and the world is still going to go round whether you believe in Him or not!" He was greatly relieved. His level of projection was such that he thought if he didn't think God existed, God stopped existing. C S Lewis writes, *"The prayer preceding all prayers is, 'May it be the real Thou that I speak to.'"*[24]

What is God really like?

Psalm 1:1-3: *"Blessed is the one who does not walk in step with the wicked or stand in the way that sinners take or sit in the company of mockers, but whose delight is in the law of the Lord, and who meditates on His law day and night. That person is like a tree planted by streams of water, which yields its fruit in season and whose leaf does not wither."*

This psalm begins with the word 'blessed', or 'happy', which in Hebrew is *ashrei*. Like many Hebrew words, it derives its meaning from its relation to the word *asker*, which means 'being on the road 'or 'going straight'. The essence of Judaism is a rhythm of worship and right living which helps us to be blessed. This happy person is like a tree planted by streams of water, where leaves never wither – green leaves in drought – and it bears fruit in season. "This gives me a picture of a man being like a 'walking tree', walking straight, drawing life and peace from the living water."[25] We all want fathers like this – strong, reliable, safe.

I used to have a fairy story book with a picture of an oak tree with a door in the trunk called "The Magic of the Faraway Tree" by Enid Blyton. I wanted to live in there, inside somewhere, protected, safe, that would provide a place where the branches pointed upwards to God. This is how fathers are meant to be. However, this is not what we always experience, and therefore what one part of our mind knows about Father God – usually through scripture –does not correlate with our experience of our earthly Dads.

The left side of our brain (known as our 'head') specialises in analysis, language and problem-solving; it suppresses information it cannot grasp conceptually or that 'doesn't fit'. The right hemisphere of the brain (our 'heart') is essential for the creation of poetry, art and for symbolic ways of knowing. It is comfortable with parable and metaphor, whereas our left side tends to be more literal. The right side is sensitive to and aware of relationships. It absorbs and records atmosphere and facial and body language, even when these pressures and tensions do not fit with the words being spoken. This relates to what is commonly called the 'split between the head and heart'.

This symbolic way of knowing is one of the reasons Jesus spoke in parables, nudging us towards receptive insight – intending to stimulate intense thought. In Hebrew history, it was often the preferred way of teaching. Parables move us beyond intellectual ability. Jesus, when teaching with stories, was speaking to the right hemisphere – to the spiritual eyes and ears of our heart.

Just one more foundational understanding as we explore the heart of God, whom Jesus referred to as Father. It is important to be clear that God is not limited to gender. God is not male or female. In Genesis 1:26-27, God created humanity in His image, male and female. So, while God is not male or female, there is something about women and men together that reveals the image of God. And as God is not limited to gender, God as divine parent is not limited to being Father. However, in this book I will generally refer to God as 'God the Father'.

With this in mind, I have found four main false images people tend to have of God. This very much reflects Brad Jersak's teaching in his book, "A More Christlike God" and in addition I have written on the distorted image of God from a different perspective in "Father Matters".

1. The angry God

The angry God must be placated, kept happy and sacrificed to. Nowadays this doesn't mean burnt offerings, of course, but striving to do good works or enduring the burden of attending meetings, for example. It gives rise to such questions as, 'Have I done enough? Given away enough money? What else do I need to do?' This slips into having to keep the eldership – who represent God – happy. As Gerard Hughes writes: *"Fred was considered a model Christian. He was young, married and, in addition to his professional work he belonged to several voluntary bodies, took an intelligent interest in theology, lived a very simple lifestyle, rarely dining out or going to films or theatre, and he and his wife spent most of their holiday times at conferences. On one of his holidays, he came to make an individually given retreat. I encouraged him to pray by using his imagination on scenes from the gospel, entering the scene as though it were happening and himself a participant. At the end of each day he would tell me what he had experienced in these scenes. One day he had been imagining the marriage feast at Cana. He had a vivid imagination and had seen tables heaped with food set out beneath a blue sky. The guests were dancing and it was a scene of great merriment. 'Did you see Christ?' I asked. 'Yes,' he said, 'Christ was sitting upright on a straight-backed chair, clothed in a white robe, a staff in his hand, a crown of thorns on his head, looking disapproving.'"[26]*

The imagination is a wonderful and much neglected faculty. It enables us to enter into the scenes of the gospel with our senses and our feelings, as well as with our minds, but it also projects into our conscious minds thoughts, memories and feelings. These, although partially hidden from deep in our hearts, have, in fact, been influencing our perception, thinking and acting. In Fred's case, this image of Christ revealed much to him about his basic image of God and of Christ which had been hidden from him earlier. Before praying using this Cana scene, if he had been asked, "What is your basic notion of God and of Christ?" he would probably have answered, "God is the God of love, mercy and compassion." Deep down in his heart another image of God was effectively operating and influencing his life.

As he reflected on this image of the disapproving Christ, he began to understand many things in his own life. He saw a Christ who disapproved of merriment, who demanded an unceasing application to good works; a tyrannical Christ who did not permit the simple pleasures of life. He began to realise that he had never allowed himself to admit the truth that he really experienced no joy or rest in his multiple commitments to good works. He felt constantly guilty and driven by a demanding and angry God. The more he was advised – and advised himself – to rest in God's peace, the worse he felt, but the 'oughts' in his life were so strong that he continued to strive.

If a false, angry, tyrannical image of God is operating, all encouragement to return to the Father, at a deep level, means, 'Return to your tyrant'. I sometimes call this angry, false god, the 'monster' god. We are left striving, having to be the good girl/boy and avoiding getting into trouble. Depending on personality, it means avoiding too much responsibility so that we are not the victim to others' or God's perceived anger when things go wrong, or we over-commit to avoid facing our heart's misgivings. Certainly not a place of rest.

Hosea 6:6 (MSG): *"I'm after love that lasts, not more religion. I want you to know God, not go to more prayer meetings."*

2. The distant/silent God

A faceless, cosmic force that launched the world but leaves it alone. This was my 'distorted image'. It makes us believe that God is indifferent to us, not interested in us. We are a faceless 'blob', and, as long as the Kingdom work is done, it doesn't matter much who does it. It causes feelings that we have been left to make the best of it, that we're overlooked and not listened to. We lack personal identity; we're lost and need to be self-sufficient. Life is to be negotiated but there is no clear guidance as to how; no 'map' to help us through, and because we have lived with emotional 'rationing', we settle for little and have low expectations.

I was at a conference once and we were asked to get into twos or threes and ask God to speak to us for a 'word' for each other. This lady had the word 'favourite', then immediately added, "But I know God has no favourites?" What she did not know was that, although my father loved me, he did not particularly like me; my sister was his favourite. This word from God was therefore immensely healing. I did not mind that everyone else was God's favourite, as long as I was as well!

My mantra now is, 'God is always good, and I am always loved.'

3. The critical God

When we are children, we see our parents as godlike. They have the capacity to bless or to curse us. We internalise critical words; we criticise ourselves and project all of this onto God. The critical God is also demanding. There are conditions to his acceptance of us and He is capricious and may change His mind. This leaves us feeling very unsafe, continually striving to earn His approval, not trusting our own abilities. We have resigned ourselves to the fact that we will never please God. He wants perfection. There will always be something to criticise.

We live in a performance-orientated world. Will we be good enough to make the football team? Are we pretty enough? Will we get into university?

We think God is like this. But He is not! God sets us up for achievement, not failure. He is pleased with us, not disappointed. When we have lived like this, and believe God to be like this, we experience negative self-talk and lack of self-acceptance – never being good enough. We may come from homes where there is confusion, where the goalposts move. If you come from a family with alcoholic parents, sometimes you are not allowed to do something and rage explodes all over you. Then, another time, no-one notices your behaviour. God does not change. He is constant, unchanging, and His decisions are according to what is best for us, not according to how He feels that day.

4. The indulgent God

This really is the most dangerous and difficult false image of God, because it is the nearest to the truth, in that He is loving, but it lacks the whole picture. This God is indulgent and will answer all our prayers in the way we expect him to, so when things go wrong the person feels unloved and abandoned. This is an entitlement message which leaves little room for the concept of suffering. We see God as a sentimental, indulgent, 'Father Christmas' figure.[27] This false image enters our lives occasionally to give us presents. He is nice to have around if everything is going well, but when disaster strikes, or our wish fulfilment is delayed, we give up believing in Him. This is particularly true where we have heard a 'victorious living' type of gospel, in which there is no room for a 'suffering servant' image of God. The emphasis on everything is resurrected, victorious living with no need for perseverance, let alone 'a long obedience in the same direction'.

We, or others, may negate the indulgent God with an anti-grace message. Our Father Christmas or Fairy Godmother view of God becomes conditional: in just the same way you have been told to be a good boy/girl or Father Christmas won't bring you any presents, God keeps a list of your sins. Sin does not separate us from the love of God, but from clear communication with Him.

We can ask this 'Father Christmas' god for anything we want

– send our list to the 'North Pole' ("Ask anything in my Name and I will do it") but we risk disappointment when the present isn't quite right. Yet we know we have to be grateful and say thank you anyway. This creates a hybrid theology whereby we ask, hoping our faith is good enough, followed by disappointment with an unanswered prayer; having faith in faith rather than faith in a loving, caring God. This echoes our distorted image of the distant God, who lives far away and only visits at Christmas (while you are asleep) or the divorced father image of God who visits, bringing gifts, then disappears; a God who lives in heaven – further than the North Pole – and is coming again someday like a thief in the night.

However, God is like *Jesus.* Brad Jersak, quoting Peter Fitch, writes: *"Jesus came from His Father into the world to reveal God in a way we could see, hear and touch. Imagine the God of the universe, who dwells in unapproachable light but if you had a smartphone you could have posed for a 'selfie' with Him. Astonishing!"*[28]

The Word became flesh

John 1:1-5 (NRSV): *"In the beginning was the Word, and the Word was with God, and the Word was God. He was in the beginning with God. All things came into being through him, and without him not one thing came into being. What has come into being in him was life, and the life was the light of all people. The light shines in the darkness, and the darkness did not overcome it."*

John 1:1-5 (MSG): *"The Word was first, the Word present to God, God present to the Word. The Word was God, in readiness for God from day one. Everything was created through him; nothing – not one thing! – came into being without him. What came into existence was Life, and the Life was Light to live by. The Life-Light blazed out of the darkness; The darkness couldn't put it out."*

The opening verses of John's gospel are probably some of the most beautiful and well-known words of the whole Bible, often read at Christmas in services and accompanied by well-known carols. They create a mixture of familiarity along with holiness and wonder. Yet at the time when it was written this opening statement disturbed both Jew and Greek. To the Greeks 'the Word', which was translated 'Logos', was used to describe the pagan notion of divinity, a divine philosophy. To the Jews the idea of God being linked to flesh was viewed as carnal. The Jews had over six hundred rules segregating holiness from worldliness.

The eternal 'Word' became flesh and spoke in a regional accent, with the full range of physical limitations and human emotions, with flesh that endured suffering; the Word, the Alpha and Omega and all the letters in between.

Christ holds it all together

Colossians 1:15-18 (MSG): *"We look at this Son and see the God who cannot be seen. We look at this Son and see God's original purpose in everything created. For everything, absolutely everything, above and below, visible and invisible, rank after rank after rank of angels – EVERYTHING got started in him and finds its purpose in him. He was there before any of it came into existence and holds it all together right up to this moment. And when it comes to the church, he organises and holds it together, like a head does a body."*

This, in essence, says that when we look at Jesus we see God: not a bit of God, not an aspect of God, not a public relations representation of God. We see *God*. Authentic humanity.

Colossians 2:9-11 (MSG): *"Everything of God gets expressed in him, so you can see and hear him clearly. You don't need a telescope, a microscope to realise the fullness of Christ and the emptiness of the universe without him. When you come to him, that fullness comes together for you, too. His power extends over everything. Entering into this fullness is not something you figure out or achieve."*

John's first letter continues with this essential truth:

"From the very first day, we were there, taking it all in – we heard it with our own ears, saw it with our own eyes, verified it with our own hands. The Word of Life appeared right before our eyes; we saw it happen! And now we're telling you in most sober prose that what we witnessed was, incredibly, this: The infinite Life of God himself took shape before us. We saw it, we heard it and now we're telling you so you can experience it along with us, this experience of communion with the Father and his Son, Jesus Christ. Our motive for writing is simply this: We want you to enjoy this, too. Your joy will double our joy!" 1 John 1:1-4 (MSG)

The apostles had seen God, heard God and touched God, but after years of walking with him it was still a struggle for them to come into the revelation of Jesus. We see this in John 14:1-3 (NRSV): *"Do not let your hearts be troubled. Believe in God, believe also in Me. In my Father's house there are many dwelling places. If it were not so, would I have told you that I go to prepare a place for you? And if I go and prepare a place for you, I will come again and take you to myself, so that where I am, there you may be also."*

Jesus is saying, "Trust Me, don't have troubled hearts, trust and rest in the truth, I have your eternal future all planned out for you." As we understand more of what the original words mean, we start to glimpse what a beautiful promise Jesus is making.

The word for 'dwelling place', *mon-ai* in the Greek, has a primary meaning of a place to stay, tarry, abide or dwelling. A home. John 14:2 has the idea that Jesus is going to make a home for us which includes a heavenly assignment. He is saying I am going ahead of you to plan a glorious future in which you can continually abide and rest with me. And this becomes even more of a promise in verse 3, where Jesus says, "I will come again and take you to myself." The word here is *paralambano* which was the word used for a bridegroom taking his bride. And for the listeners this would have resonated with God's marriage covenant with Israel.

Exodus 6:7 (NKJV): *"I will take you as a people, and I will be your God. Then you shall know I am the Lord your God who brings you out from under the burdens of Egypt."*

So Jesus is going to plan a joint future for Himself as the Bridegroom and us as His Bride. Thomas, having heard this says, in essence, "We have no idea where you are going." Jesus replies (John 14:6-8), *"I am the Way the Truth and the Life. No-one comes to the Father except through Me. If you really know Me, you would know My Father as well. From now on, you do know Him and have seen Him."* Then the apostle Philip asked him, *"Show us the Father and that will be enough for us."* Jesus himself declared, *"Don't you know me, Philip, even after I have been among you such a long time? Anyone who has seen me has seen the Father."* (John 14:9). *"I and the Father are one,"* He says (John 10:30).

If we really believe Jesus' all-embracing statement as to who He is, it has the potential to initiate also a radical reshaping of the image of God in our hearts. Former Archbishop of

Canterbury, Michael Ramsey, once said, *"God is Christlike and in Him there is no un-Christlikeness at all."*

Whilst Brian Zahnd, in a sermon said, *"God is like Jesus. God has always been like Jesus. There has never been a time when God was not like Jesus. We have not always known what God is like. But now we do. God does not change and is not subject to change. Jesus does not change God. Jesus reveals God."*

This is not a God to run from, but to rest in.

This intimate relationship Jesus is inviting us into, with Him as the bridegroom, also includes an invitation into the warmth of the Father's heart. He invites us into a relationship, not into an abstract doctrine, but to a divine life shaped by grace. A relationship with the Trinity, a God of grace, a God who saves, the Lord, the Giver of life. At the heart of the doctrine of God as Trinity is the conviction that God is a communion of persons; a divine dance of mutual indwelling love, which we are invited to join.

Jesus' favourite name for God is 'Father'. Jesus calls God *Father* seventy times in the gospels. To call God 'Abba', meaning 'dearest Papa' or 'Daddy', is a truly radical statement. This would have been alarming to those who first heard it. The nearest example I can think of is to imagine someone going on television to announce to all UK residents that the King of England would like us to call him 'Daddy'.

I was meditating on Matthew 6:9, the beginning of the Lord's Prayer, where Jesus is teaching his followers how to pray. He begins, "Our Father" and, although I understand we usually think of the 'our' as the corporate response – in that we are God's children – in my picture Jesus was putting His arm around two of the disciples. In this act the 'Our Father' became Jesus joining with us as the elder brother, ushering us into our Father's presence.

LISTENING TO GOD

Why is listening so important? In John 14:15, for example, Jesus says to the disciples, *"If you love Me you will obey Me."* How do we know how to obey unless we hear? After telling parables, Jesus would say, "If you have eyes to see and ears to hear." These are the 'eyes' and 'ears' of our heart He is speaking about, our spiritual 'eyes' and 'ears'. A paraphrase of the introduction to Leanne Payne's *Listening Prayer* reads, "We live in an age of noise, confusion and hurry. Our timetables are frequently full to overflowing. What is often lost in the din is absolutely vital to our spiritual health and maturity, the still small voice of God. God speaks to us, His children, in a number of ways but, like young Samuel, we don't always recognise His voice. We don't know how to listen to our Father. True listening is obedient listening. To cross the line from spiritual immaturity to maturity we must learn to hear God's voice. Only then can we find the mind of Christ and gain wisdom, knowledge, understanding and guidance." Leanne Payne wrote that in 1974 and I would suggest that the noise, confusion and speed of life have increased significantly since then.

When we learn to listen, our lives become obedient lives. In Latin the verb to obey is *obedire*, often linked to *audire,* auditory, to hear. So we can say that to listen is to obey. In Hebrew, the word *shema* is 'to hear', as used in Deuteronomy 6:4. It has the connotation of 'hear and obey'. In fact, in Deuteronomy 6 the Lord states clearly what our mission should be: to teach our children to walk in the fear of the Lord. When Jesus reiterates this, in John's gospel, it is about it being a love response. *"If you love Me, you will keep My commandments,"* (John 14:15 NRSV). I was meditating on what this meant, and God said, "When you learn to love Me, to embrace love, you will want to do what I want for you. We will fit into love together." The Bible is our primary source.

"He is a shield unto them that put their trust in Him." (Proverbs 30:5 KJV)

"The devil is not afraid of a dust-covered Bible." Charles Spurgeon

The principles of the Bible are the groundwork of human freedom.

D L Moody: *"The Bible was not given for our information, but for our transformation."*

Immanuel Kant: *"No-one ever graduates from Bible study until he meets the Author face to face. A single line in the Bible has consoled me more than all the books I have ever read besides."*

A W Tozer: *"God did not write a book and send it by messenger to be read at a distance by unaided minds. He spoke a book and lives in His spoken words, constantly speaking His words, causing the power of them to persist across the years."*

God desires to speak into our life. He knows about the falling sparrow and the hairs on our head. That's how concerned he is for us, so surely He wants to speak to us. Let us look at how He does this.

Do not despise small beginnings, 'baby talk'. God does not move us from learning our maths tables to complex geometry in one evening. It is little by little, not immediately a four-page prophecy! A toddler from a healthy family does not wake up and think, "I hope I can hear Mummy/Daddy today. I hope I understand what they are telling me." There are no wrong or right answers. No better answers than others. And we will make lots of mistakes.

Brainstorming how God speaks

Through:
- Bible
- 'Blobs' of knowing
- Memory
- Creation
- Music
- Dreams
- Pictures
- Words
- Impressions
- Other people
- Stories
- Pain/suffering
- Audible voice
- Promptings
- Worship
- Circumstances/God-incidences
- Symbols
- Sacraments
- Children
- Prophecy
- Burdens

- The arts – music, books, films, plays, theatre, paintings, dance, mime
- Prayer
- History
- Conscience
- Words of knowledge
- Theophanies
- Wisdom

Some examples of His speaking

The Bible

God obviously speaks through the Bible. As I have already written, I am not criticising studying and learning what the Bible means, but I think God does speak when His Holy Spirit feeds the words back to us. Then we begin to understand the Bible not so much as a map and a textbook, but as living supernatural nourishment we feed from. It is revelation. The Holy Spirit can actually take words and feed them to us, much like bread and wine, and it is at that level that we may experience the written word as God speaking to us. We can read something that we have read many times before, but the Holy Spirit will highlight it in such a way that all of a sudden we will see five words staring at us as though we have never seen them before, having all new meaning and new life to them.

A 'blob of knowing'

For lots of people His speaking comes through what Clay McLean describes as a 'blob of knowing'. It is not defined, it is not a lovely scripture, it is not a definite picture, it is just a gut feeling of knowing – you *know* that you know God is speaking. Unfortunately, most people who do talks or write books aren't the 'blobs of knowing' kind of people, because we haven't really got an awful lot to say if we admit, "Well I generally get the idea of what God wants me to do by this blob of knowing." There are lots of people who are like that; they get a gut reaction as to what God is saying to them and what He wants them to do (revelation).

Memory

God speaks through our memory by bringing to mind what is important. This is something we have not treasured in the western world. We are very 'instant'. We have instant coffee, instant Internet access etc, and we are not used to planting a seed and waiting for it to grow. We are not used to keeping the good things that God has done for us in our memory. We often do not really know how to build our own faith from such memories.

I used to wonder why the Old Testament prayers began with, *"...and You, God, brought us out of Egypt ... and You ..."*, and they would go through a long history of God's encounters with them before they prayed. Now I know they did it to build up each other's faith. Maybe we could learn to do that for ourselves, for example, declaring, "You did this for me and that for me", and hold in our memories those things that God has done for us that are good, and bring them to mind. I remember once, in a desperate situation, that I prayed that God would do something, and I remember, as it happened, I said to Him, "I will trust You always; I will never doubt You again". Two days later, I could remember saying it but I could not remember why! It had gone, because many of us don't know how to develop our memories in these areas. This incident is what prompted me to start a journal. As I have written elsewhere, we tend to remember what we need to forget and forget what we need to remember. And Satan steals seeds and stifles the growth as illustrated in the parable of the sower (Matthew 13).

Creation

God speaks through creation. I used to miss this completely. Before I was a Christian, people would say, "You must know there is a God – look at that tree", or "Look at that sunset", and I used to say, "It doesn't do anything for me. I like people." I was the centre of my world. I saw things through the grid of whether it did anything for me. No, it didn't speak to me. It was a revelation when I suddenly realised creation was saying something about the Creator. Very often we are self-centred, but when we start to hear Him speak to us through creation we start to think, "Oh, God must be like that as well, that must be something of His character." He also speaks to us through daily living and through experience. Once, when I was in Geneva, I spent the morning looking at jewellery in the many shops. There were beautiful, magnificent diamonds. I then went to Lake Geneva and watched the sun playing with the water, creating 'liquid diamonds' – diamonds that could dance!

Music

God speaks through music, including rock and roll, I might add! We once sat in church and sang *Blessed be the Name of the Lord* to a really rocky beat for quite a long time, and I actually had the whole shape of a talk coming into my mind! Once, when listening to classical music on a balmy summer evening at an outdoor event, God gave me the whole shape of an intercessory prayer plan for a charity.

Dreams

God invariably speaks to me through dreams. Not every dream I have had is from God of course, but sometimes I wake up and think, "What was that about?" and it is often something I am unwilling to face in my heart. When my head is 'turned off' from censoring, whilst I am asleep, my heart brings up any fears in the subconscious in some form of symbolised dream. The following are examples.

When our youngest first went to work, Ron, my husband, was getting him a job in an office and I really hadn't caught up with how well our youngest son had developed. (He really should have still been in a cot as far as I was concerned!) It felt extremely silly that he was having to go to work! I had two dreams quickly following one another. In both dreams I had my youngest in a carrycot and in one dream my husband Ron was putting me on the bus, saying, "That's the bus for Harrod's," and as I sat down, I saw the bus for Harrod's going the other way.

In the other one, I was left at an airport by Ron with my baby in a carrycot and he said, "Oh, I think your flight is up next, but I have got to rush," and my flight never came up. When I awoke, I realised I was not trusting at all that a job could ever be found and, anyway, he wasn't old enough. There I was with my carrycot in all these scary situations on a bus going in the wrong direction and at an airport with no flight number coming up, and that is really how I felt. I had to pray and let go and trust.

In another situation, back in the late seventies or early eighties, I was listening to a well-known, respected Christian leader speaking against inner healing. He felt it created unhealthy dependency between the prayer minister and the person receiving prayer (which can be true) and that it opened a 'can of worms' unnecessarily, as everything we needed was in the cross (true, but part of inner healing is learning how to appropriate this) and the Kingdom needed to be advanced.

Again, I had two dreams in fairly quick succession. In the first dream I was the leader of an army hospital. I had lots of patients with invisible wounds who initially got worse, often having operations they didn't know they needed. I was speaking with the leader of the army (who was the critical speaker the previous day), agreeing that we should march again, but said that my hospital staff and patients would be much slower. In the second dream, I saw people crawling out of the desert, so weak from lack of water that they were unable to stand. Many were going out to meet them with small cups of water. This activity continued day after day. The recipients were very grateful. Behind the givers of the water I saw a fountain, the source of the water, but this was blocked by the helpers.

These two dreams profoundly affected how I ministered. I recognised that other leaders had very different gifts and priorities and we could work together, but there needed to be a fresh understanding and language that made sense to different members of the Body of Christ. Secondly, I understood that when we ministered, we must be careful to introduce others to the source of life – Jesus – not *be* their source of life.

Once, before a visiting speaker came to the UK, I had this dream. The speaker was given a car by an organisation for a tour which went through lots of hilly country, but the brakes weren't working. He managed to navigate the car brilliantly by continually going into reverse to slow it down. When he arrived at the conference, I told him the dream. It described accurately how his administration staff in the USA were failing and how he was forever having to 'back track' to sort things out.

This is a word of knowledge given in a dream before an HPS conference. On a Friday night I had a dream of a sheriff/leader giving a star to someone very unsuitable. The star burnt into their shoulder, and I knew in the dream that the star both burdened them and shaped their identity. The following morning during the ministry time, I asked if anyone felt burdened or shaped by any leadership or promotion to come forward. No-one did. However, at lunch time, a young man arrived for lunch literally announcing he was the leader of one of the congregations of 300. Several team members of both HPS and the host church team who knew him, came up to me saying that he was the 'star man'.

Again, in a dream about five years ago, I was asking Jesus to come and help me with the script for a play I was involved in. Jesus said yes, He would, or I could join Him in His play with His script. I woke up instantly and was scared rather than excited because I didn't know what it entailed.

My Bible reading that morning was Psalm 127, *"Unless the Lord builds the house those its builders labour in vain."* The following night I heard the words, "The CDs are not in my script." At that time we sold CDs of the Healing Prayer School talks, which made us some money in royalties, but I stopped them immediately. Following that step, God, in His faithfulness, made sure we did not financially miss out and He met our needs in both small and large matters (such as the use of a villa in Portugal free of charge, for example). Quite soon after that some aspects of the HPS Team changed and CDs began to be a thing of the past as we started to release mp3s through the website.

Words of knowledge

Another way God speaks to us is through 'words of knowledge', sometimes called 'words of wisdom'. They can be for others and are very similar to prophecy. The Healing Prayer School team meets every Thursday evening with the primary intention of listening to God. From these meetings, and all the words of knowledge we receive, I am able to structure the lectures for an event in such a way that they are 'tailor-made' rather than 'off the peg'. However, words of knowledge are not necessarily always given in structured prayer times. Here are some examples of both.

The very first significant word of knowledge I had was when my prayer partner and I visited a lady who wanted to join one of the daytime Young Wives' group the church was running at the time. The lady was married to a well-respected Christian government leader. Whilst we were talking, the thought I had was, "He is physically violent". I dismissed the thought. The next morning, she rang me and said, "You know, don't you?" I decided to risk believing my thought and said, "Yes". And it was true.

I also meet with a group of ladies on a Monday afternoon. One week Helen said she had been praying for a girl, Christine, a young wife in our church congregation who had suffered three or four miscarriages. Helen said God had told her that Christine would have a son and name him Samuel. We decided to not tell anyone (like Mary in Luke 2:19 NLT, *"But Mary quietly treasured these things in her heart and thought about them often"*). In due course Christine became pregnant again and went full term. As she was giving birth God said to her, "Name him Samuel!"

Another time I was standing behind a member of our church at a cash machine. The thought dropped into my mind, "She is having an affair." She turned to me, and we started chatting and then she looked at me and said, "You know, don't you?" This time, as this was quite a few years later, my "Yes" was more confident. We arranged to meet to pray. God was wanting to rescue her.

Sometimes God uses these words of knowledge to illustrate how we can all continually listen to Him. I was at a Ladies' Day Conference as the main speaker for the afternoon. During the second half of the morning there were different activities to choose from. I went to a lecture on beauty vitamins. As an icebreaker, the speaker passed around a book which contained a photograph of a woman whose age we had to guess. I prayed and asked God how old she was. We then wrote a number on a piece of paper with our name, folded it and put it in a basket. At the end of the morning the speaker went through the bits of paper. There were thirty to forty of us attending and mine was the only correct answer. I told them what I had done.

Often it isn't only the word of knowledge that is so amazing, it is how God orchestrates everything for the person to get the word. A few years ago, when I was head of the ministry team at a New Wine week, on the first night (Saturday) a lady came up to me saying she had given a particular word of knowledge to the leadership, but it had not been read out. The word was for 'Caroline' but spelt with a 'K'. "You have not made a mistake," I assured her and said that if I saw 'Karoline' I would give her the message (there were about five thousand people attending the arena each evening). Another evening a lady came forward to me for prayer and her badge read 'Karoline'. I gave her God's message, which was extremely meaningful to her, and I said it should have been read out on Saturday evening. "Oh" she said, "I didn't arrive until Sunday!" I then wanted to tell the person who had received the word all about it but couldn't remember what she looked like. On the last evening, she found me, and I was able to tell her not only had she not made a mistake, but neither had the person on the platform!

My last story is when I was the speaker at a women's brunch. Three years ago, the last time I had been speaking there, I received a word of knowledge for someone with a pain in the centre of their chest. A lady had come forward who had cancer, which was being well controlled by medication but the pain had begun to worsen. We prayed and she had decided to go back to her doctor. So on this return visit, I was wondering how she was but couldn't remember her name or what she looked like. The only vague fact I had to go on was a thought that she might have had one or two daughters. At this venue everyone was sitting at tables of eight. I chose a table along with one of my friends and a lady near me said, "You won't remember me but ..." and proceeded to tell me how she was still well because the pain indicated that the medication needed adjusting.

Why am I writing all these stories? Because, as we learn to listen to God and to rest in Him, it doesn't mean that our 'rest-life' will be 'grey' and without purpose. It means that as we grow in the 'unforced rhythms of grace' we will experience life-giving opportunities to be involved in the Kingdom. No striving, just resting.

Theophanies

Theophany is a personal encounter with a deity, that is, an event where the manifestation of a deity occurs in an observable way. Specifically, it refers to the temporal and spatial manifestation of God in some tangible form. Theophany means 'God's in-breaking'. *"Then Jacob awoke from his sleep and said, 'Surely the Lord is in this place, and I wasn't even aware of it.'"* Genesis 28:16 (NLT)

In order to be aware of this, we need to have the eyes and ears of our hearts cleansed and opened to be able to see God's in-breaking into the physical world. It also takes practice. Last Christmas I visited the new World Trade Center development in New York. One of the first things our guide showed us was the Survivor Tree. Here's the story:

"In October 2001, recovery workers, sifting through the rubble of the destroyed World Trade Center, uncovered the remains of a Callery pear tree. Twisted and broken, its roots had snapped and its branches had burned but, unlike all the other trees, it still showed some signs of life. The workers decided to pull the tree from the ground in the hope of its recovery, and then it was sent for specialist care. It was not expected to survive. For several years the tree underwent a careful process of healing and rehabilitation. In 2010, nine years later, the Callery pear tree was returned to the World Trade Center site. It was christened, 'The Survivor Tree', a symbol of endurance, resilience and hope. Since its return there, the tree has flourished. It is often the first tree to bloom in the 9/11 Memorial Plaza each year, signalling the arrival of spring, with an annual display of growth and rebirth. At the same time the Survivor Tree bears the scars of its troubled past. Its smooth new branches reach upwards from its gnarled stump, a stark reminder of its dark history and its hopeful present." So, listening to the guide, I was also aware that this was a theophany moment, and I was reminded of verse 7 in Job 14, *"There is hope for a tree: If it is cut down, it will sprout again, and its new shoots will not fail."* And then I thought, what a wonderful description of us! We can be twisted, broken, snapped or burned, but in the loving hands of God our Father, we are healed and rehabilitated, bearing the scars of our troubled past but still flourishing with newness of life, reaching upwards towards God.

Whilst still dwelling on all that God was saying through the tree, the guide went on to talk about a fireboat called *John J Harvey*. Launched in 1931, it served as a firefighter boat with a distinguished career until 1994, when at auction it was being sold for scrap. A private consortium for marine preservation bought it, determined to save it from the scrap heap. She was restored and hosted frequent free trips on the River Hudson. On the morning of September 11th, 2001, following the collapse of the second of the twin towers, firefighters had ascertained that the vast scale of destruction had damaged many fire mains, depriving the fire crews of water. Officials radioed the *Harvey* asking if her pumps still worked. Responding that they did, the crew was told to drop off her passengers and return to the disaster site. Up until this point the *Harvey*, like many other small ships on the Hudson, was rescuing people. She returned and pumped water at the site for eighty hours until the water mains were restored.

An amazing story in itself, but, again, how like so many Bible stories and ours. Taken into exile, left in prison 'and yet'. Which can be like us; overlooked and not valued until someone sees who we really are or what we were like, or have achieved, and gives us purpose again. I have prayed with many people who were told by parents that they would 'never amount to anything', but this is not how God sees us. Jeremiah 29:11 reads, *"For I know the plans I have for you,"* *declares the Lord, "plans to prosper you and not to harm you, plans to give you hope and a future."*

Not all theophanies are that formal. Many are being acted out in our everyday ordinary lives. I was sitting round a swimming pool watching two brothers about 10 and 14 years old. As they left the pool, the older brother said, "Throw your beach ball back in the pool. You can't take it on the plane with you." The younger one wasn't happy about this but after a slightly sterner instruction, did so. A little girl immediately grabbed it, and the older brother said, "See, you made someone happy."

I then watched them go to settle what I assumed was the bar bill (presumably under parental instructions) and the older brother, trying to appear very grown up, was handing over the room number whilst dangling one foot in the paddling pool. The younger brother looked up and dangled one of his feet in the pool. I thought, yes, sometimes we obey somewhat reluctantly but this doesn't work; we become resentful about keeping the rules until we can look up at someone we adore and want to copy them.

Another illustration of this was during lockdown. A young boy of 8 or 9 years old had obviously been given the job of posting a letter. Where he had posted it at an angle, it had got stuck, so he was standing on tiptoe trying to blow it in. I assume he had been told not to touch anything, so this was his solution. I saw that he was trusting his parents' instructions and continuing to obey even though he had to persevere with an ingenious solution. Another God moment – another theophany.

Back to Ground Zero in New York, the most chilling, yet awe-inspiring theophany from that time takes no interpretation. This is what I saw, and this story is the background.
In March 2002, a firefighter sifting through the rubble of Ground Zero made a remarkable discovery: a Bible fused to

a chunk of steel. The firefighter gave the treasure to Joel Meyerowitz, who was the official photographer. Meyerowitz was totally speechless when his eyes fell upon the Bible verse exposed on the surface of what he called, 'heart-shaped' steel. Under a section entitled 'Retaliation' was the verse: *"Ye have heard that it hath been said, an eye for an eye and a tooth for a tooth but I say unto you, that you resist not evil, but whosoever shall smite thee on thy right cheek, turn to him the other also."*

Here is God breathing; speaking into modern history and, quoting the internet, "May this word be seared on our heart as securely as this page was fused to steel."[29]

BARRIERS TO HEARING GOD

Inability to rest

Our society teaches us that non-productive time is a waste of time. Yet it is often in the 'doing nothing' time that we can hear God and enjoy being with Him. This poem expresses it well:

I wasted an hour one morning beside a mountain stream.
I seized a cloud from the sky above and fashioned myself a dream.
In the hush of early twilight, far from the haunts of men,
I wasted a summer evening and fashioned my dream again.
Wasted? Perhaps.
Folks say so who have never walked with God ...
When lanes are purple with lilacs or yellow with goldenrod.
But I have found strength for my labours
In that one short evening hour.
I have found joy and contentment.
I have found peace and power.

My dreaming has left me a treasure,
A hope that is strong and true.
From wasted hours I have built my life and found my faith
anew.

Author unknown

Being too busy – always being on the go – blocks us from hearing God's voice. Remember Jesus commended Mary for sitting, for 'being' rather than Martha's restless fussing. We need to develop a still, calm heart that can wait with expectation that our loving Heavenly Father will speak to us. Once, Ron (my husband) and I went to collect some American friends from a London hotel to take them to the airport. As Ron was driving down the road he saw their son James racing down the road behind us. Ron pulled over and stopped. When James arrived he could not speak for a minute or so, he was so out of breath. His parents had left their passports in the hotel room. I thought this was such an illustration of how we have to wait for our hearts to calm down, to catch up after we have been rushing, busy.

A friend of mine, Harry Sutton, a worldwide evangelist and missionary, would sometimes say, "I am going to bed for the afternoon to let my soul catch up with my body." This busyness, of course, need not be physical. It may be in our minds. How many of us have been in church worshipping or listening to the sermon only to have our minds distracted by a shopping list, what we will be eating following the service or who we need to ring? We can be so busy that it becomes almost impossible to practise the presence of Jesus. There is barely any room for God, and when we try to stop and open our hearts to Him, all the concerns and 'to dos' of life come rushing in. Henri Nouwen wrote: *"... we, busy with many things, begin to seek after the small, flighty sensations brought about by artificial stimulation of the senses."*[30]

I have learned some of the areas where I can become distracted (they are different for all of us). For example, I have learned not to go shopping – even window shopping – whilst at a conference. I came to understand this weakness many years ago at a John Wimber conference in Brighton. A small group of us had wandered around the shops at lunchtime, an innocent pursuit, and probably fine for everyone else! However, when the afternoon session started with wonderful worship, different outfits kept floating across my mind and I found myself thinking of how they would go with various shoes or jackets I had at home. I love clothes; I was a fashion model and God has given me great freedom to express this part of myself, but I have had to learn how to be careful and disciplined in that area. Do I want to worship God rather than think about clothes? Of course I do! Your weaknesses and temptations will be different from mine, but we need to recognise our vulnerabilities. The enemy's desire is to exploit them, and we need to take appropriate action.

Once during a time of worship in a charismatic meeting once, I stood between Ron and a wonderful 'full-on' lover of God on the other side. I knew God loved this person very much and delighted in his worship. I knew not to judge him because, like me, he really couldn't sing! Ron, on the other hand, had a lovely voice. So I put my finger in my ear (this man didn't notice because he was lost in wonder) and leaned towards Ron to hear him. As I did this God said to me, "That's how you need to listen to me. Block out the distractions of the world and lean into me."

Lack of expectation that God speaks

Christianity is about knowing God, and central to that knowing is prayer. If, by prayer, we think only of our part, that is, how we worship, praise, petition, intercede and give thanksgiving, then it is a very one-sided affair. At the heart of Christianity is relationship because God, as triune, is always relational. We, as His children, become part of this family, and may join the conversation. However, we do not always experience this in our own prayer life or in prayer meetings. I once returned from a prayer meeting which had felt like a large number of people all speaking through the voice end of a telephone, yet no-one had been holding the phone to either ear, or even acting as though there was anyone at the other end of the telephone waiting to speak! We often pray with a megaphone! I find these meetings quite boring. I want to know what's on God's heart, to listen to Him, to receive pictures, words of knowledge or scriptures, for example.

We have lost the knowledge that we need to listen and, in the absence of that, remain disconnected and restless. We often fear silence and the quietening of our hearts that is needed to be able to listen. Dallas Willard writes, *"Silence is frightening because it strips us as nothing else does, throwing us upon the stark realities of life."*[31] This fear is well illustrated in Mark 9:2-8, which is the story of when Jesus takes Peter, James and John to a high mountain by themselves. Here Jesus is transfigured and talks with Elijah and Moses. Something exciting had happened, something outside of Peter's comfort zone, so he wanted to get busy and make three tents and dwellings. In verse 6 it says that Peter did not know what to say because he was terrified. Peter was still speaking when a cloud overshadowed them and God's voice spoke from the cloud, *"This is my dearly beloved Son – always listen to Him."* Mark 9:7 (TPT)

Seeking a place away from distraction, where we can be at rest and hear God's voice, can be called a mixture of silence and solitude. The Spiritual Formation Bible uses these definitions:

Solitude: the creation of an open, empty space in our lives by purposefully abstaining from interaction with other human beings so that, freed from competing loyalties, we can be found by God.

Silence: closing off our souls from 'sounds', whether noise, music or words, so that we may better still and silence the inner chatter and clatter of our noisy hearts and be increasingly attentive to God.

A word of caution here: start small – big picture, small step. Maybe try fifteen minutes just on your own, listening. But this listening doesn't have to be on your own. Solitude is where God shapes this gift, but *together* we can practise listening.

As I have written, the Healing Prayer School's teaching is based on what God has spoken to us. Once in The Netherlands I was teaching on the same subject in two churches on two consecutive days. Given that, the hosts assumed the teaching on Day two would be the same as for Day one, therefore they only recorded Day one! To their dismay, Day two was different, even with different team members teaching, because we knew that God would be speaking different truths into the lives of those attending.

A church leader who had attended both days asked me where I had researched the church history of The Netherlands, as I "Obviously understood the influence of ... in that area as opposed to the other area." I hadn't! As a group, we had listened to God and attempted to obey.

Some of us have a low or no expectation that God will speak to us because we are insecure in our identity. We will look at this more in another Chapter. Even if our family overlooks or ignores us, God doesn't. We are unique, worthy of attention, priceless. The Lord will never make another you. You are created for a purpose that only you can fulfil (Ephesians 2:10). You can't be someone else and someone else can't be you. We are all different, like colours of the rainbow. Being different does not mean being more or less than.

Needing the 'eyes and ears' of our heart cleansed

When I first became a Christian, all I wanted to do was to hear God. I knew people went to church to pray. I did not realise God answered them! So I prayed that I would have ears to hear a *loud* voice! (The still, small voice is not the only voice). When Jesus speaks about those who have eyes to see and ears to hear, He is speaking about our spiritual eyes and ears, the 'eyes' and 'ears' of our heart. Ephesians 1:18, *"I pray the eyes of your heart may be enlightened."*

We cannot listen as we would like to; we need help. Too easily today we come to prayer as if all we needed was a little more information and a little more effort and the job would be done. What we need is the same attitude as that of the Church in the early centuries of Christian discipleship. Then, when someone professed faith, the first thing the Church did was to administer deliverance. By this act the Church was dealing with the fact that the god of this age had blinded the minds of unbelievers (2 Corinthians 4:4). This included baptism by immersion, not only cleansing the person from sin, but bringing freedom from   the work of the enemy, a cleansing of our eyes and ears.

The enemy uses all sorts of tactics to try and blur and distract our vision. And if the enemy doesn't manage to disrupt everything, he tries to put us to sleep. A story that illustrates this well is the Wizard of Oz (stories are much like modern day parables: they speak eternal truths). In this familiar story, on the way to the Emerald City, Dorothy (the heroine) and her friends are hindered and menaced by the Wicked Witch of the West. She incites trees to throw apples at them and tries to set the scarecrow on fire. Within sight of the city the witch tries a more subtle approach. She conjures up a field of poppies which causes the trio to fall asleep. Glinda, the Good Witch of the North, saves them by making it snow, which counteracts the effects of the poppies.

C S Lewis writes, *"Do you think I'm trying to weave a spell? Perhaps I am. But remember your fairy tales. Spells are used for breaking enchantments as well as for inducing them, and you and I have need of the strongest spell that can be found to wake us from the evil enchantment of worldliness which has been laid upon us. Or, as the Bible says it, 'The whole world lies under the power of the evil one.' We are in a fog, we are under a spell, our hearts are shrouded, but God can come and set us free from the evil of this world, from the materialism and from the god of this world, who has blinded the eyes and ears of our hearts."*[32]

Ephesians 5:14 (NLT): *"Awake, rise, O sleeper. Rise from the dead, and Christ will give you light."*

The world's pollution has all sorts of effects on us and one of the enemy's strategies is to make access to the Father difficult. We need to learn to create our own climate, not by busyness and activity but by continuing to listen to the Father in an intimate relationship.

Henri Nouwen writes, *"I have to kneel before the Father, put my ear against His chest and listen, without interruption, to the heartbeat of God. Then, only then, can I say gently and carefully what I hear. I know now I have to speak from eternity into time, from the lasting joy into the passing realities of our short existence in this world, from the house of love into the houses of fear, from God's abode into the dwellings of human beings."*[33]

On conversion, at our baptism, we are washed clean. However, due to living in a polluted world we get dirty. It is like having cataracts that make our eyes misty. We need ongoing 'cataract operations'. The 'windscreens' of our cars need washing (the eyes and ears of our heart). I believe it is not too much of a stretch to link this with Jesus washing the disciples' feet. Jesus explains to Peter that he doesn't need to be washed all over, just where he is dirty. Resting in God's presence, with daily cleansing from the 'dust of this world', we create a 'thin place' – a place where heaven touches our world.

Clay McClean tells the story of a friend of his who had offered to chauffeur an elderly ex-missionary to China to visit some old friends who had stayed on in China. One afternoon, the three elderly missionaries sat within earshot of the chauffeur talking. One man said, *"I will be going home at Christmas"* (meaning to heaven). One of the ladies said, *"Oh, Christmas?! The Lord told me I will have to wait until Easter!"* After they left in the car the volunteer chauffeur said, *"How did they know that?"* His remaining passenger replied, *"We live in a thin place."*

And, of course, having the eyes and ears of our hearts enlightened enlarges our vision of God. Martin Luther, in a sermon he preached said, *"God writes the gospel not in the*

Bible alone, but on trees and flowers and clouds and stars." This cleansing includes what we can call 'the true imagination'. I am not going to write much here on that as there is a whole Chapter about it in my book, "Mother Matters". Suffice to say, it is an important way of seeing/knowing. Hilary Mantel once said in an interview, *"The imagination is often what converts information into implicit knowledge"* and, paraphrasing Leanne Payne, *"The true imagination is the oil on the hinge of the door which opens the way between the head and the heart."*

Not really knowing Jesus

When we know someone who is not a Christian it is very important that we understand how much God wants them to know Him. That Jesus died for everyone and there is no reluctance on God's part to speak to us. There is a story of Agnes Sanford who, when she was about to board an aeroplane, heard God tell her not to. She obeyed and the aeroplane crashed, injuring some of the passengers. When she told the story later her listeners became outraged, saying "Why was she so special that God would only save her?" "No," she said, "I was the only one listening."

God, of course, does speak to many before they actually know Him. There are many stories of how this brings people to faith. A lady came to see me for prayer for her son. I explained that she could also pray, but she was reluctant, saying she didn't really believe for herself. I hadn't seen her for about a year, when she rang me up one day after she had just been in hospital for an operation. Her story was when she came round from the operation she saw Jesus at the end of her bed, but looked away. When she looked back she saw Him again. She was very uncomfortable as she had a lot of tubes in her, was hot and sticky and her hair needed washing. She felt an absolute mess, but she kept looking at Jesus. She shut her eyes and could still see Him. She opened her eyes and thought, "What do I need to ask for?" Here was the Holy Spirit working, prompting her with the correct question. She thought, "I need to see those tubes not as my enemy but as comforting me and giving me back my life." That is what she prayed and within twenty minutes she felt different. Within those twenty minutes in hospital, the fear, panic and frustration she was experiencing in trying to lie still, all went.

The next day when she woke up, she thought, "I made all that up," but wanted to imagine Jesus again because, "Even if I had made it up, it was nice!" But she couldn't. She tried and couldn't do it. I believe this is what God does for us, whether or not we know Him. I really believe the prayers she had prayed the previous year were working in her and here we were a year later. She asked if she could come and see me because she would like me to thank God for her and I said, "You can do that yourself," and she said, "Wonderful, wonderful, I will." She later joined an Alpha group.

Being self-conscious and introspecting

We block hearing God when we introspect and turn our attention inward in order to dissect what God is maybe saying. Four of us went on a conference trip to Holland. Team member Chris Porter was reading a book with a picture of a candle on the front. Martin Tensen, who organises the conferences and is a very creative, gifted artist, sometimes decorates the hall with flowers or flowing material to symbolise a river. On arrival, this time the front of the hall was a mass of candles. During the worship time before I was due to speak, as usual, I asked God for the opening word and sentence. I felt Jesus say, "Tell them I am the Light of the

World." At this point I had a choice. I could think, "I am only thinking that because of Chris's book and all these candles, I must be making it up," or think, "This is what God has been saying all day," and just go with the flow of ideas (which I chose to do).

In *Billy Elliot*, the stage show, there is a wonderful scene where Billy is standing centre stage by himself. He has come to London to audition for the Royal Ballet but got into trouble and messed up. He stands alone on the stage but offstage the audience hears the voice of one of the judges asking Billy, *"What does it feel like, Billy? What does it feel like when you dance?"*
Billy replies, *"It's like you lose yourself – yet you feel more whole."*
(Judge): *"Just one last question. Can I ask you, Billy, what does it feel like when you're dancing?"*
(Billy): *"Don't know. Sort of feels good. It's sort of stiff and that ... but once I get going... then I, like, forget everything ... and ... sort of disappear, like I feel a change in me whole body."*

This is also an amazing description of what it is like resting and listening to the presence of God. The more you immerse yourself in God's presence, the more aware of Jesus you become and the more alive to yourself you become. Self-consciousness wrecks this.

When Ron and I were on holiday, we met a lovely couple from Switzerland. He was a professor who loved to dance. The only problem was he wasn't very good at it! One evening he was telling me how he spent his childhood in Cuba, where he learnt to tango. Talking about this, he said, "I was really quite good at it, but since I have been going to ballroom dancing lessons I can't do that either." Self-consciousness had robbed him.

A friend of mine, Chris Porter, speaks about how this is a psychological observation. We move from:

Unconscious Incompetence – we aren't even aware we can't do something
to:
Conscious Incompetence – others can do something but we can't, so we start to learn
to:
Conscious Competence – this is the 1-2-3 of dancing or the 'how to pray' instructions.

Many of us stop here, but we can move to:
Unconscious Competence – we hear the music and see the waves and surf, dance and sing, hear God's voice and live in His unforced rhythms of grace.

Romans 4:3 (MSG): *"Abraham entered into what God was doing for him, and that was the turning point. He trusted God to set him right instead of trying to be right on his own."*

Another aspect of this introspection and analysing is the worry *after* we have heard God: "Was that just my imagination? Have I made it up?" Usually it is a mixture, but we have to start somewhere! When children first go to nursery school they proudly bring home their paintings – a blob of colour, or maybe grey, as more and more paint has been applied. We say, *"Oh it is lovely, what is it?"* They reply, pointing to the coloured mess, *"This is Mummy, this is Daddy, this is the dog,"* and we answer, *"Oh of course it is, darling,"* and put it on the fridge or on the kitchen wall; not because it looks like Mummy, Daddy and the dog, but because it is a beginning, a love present, a gift in the relationship. I think some of our attempts at listening to God are pinned on 'heaven's fridge door'! When my eldest grandson was about four years old, he gave me a picture of a grey and black arch. I thanked him and asked what it was. *"It's a rainbow, Nanna."* I kept it on my desk for years. I loved it. Whenever I feel inadequate in my attempts to communicate with God, I remember Charlie's rainbow!

So whenever we find ourselves asking the question, "Was it my imagination?" it is better to ask, "Does it sound like the flesh, the unhealed self or the Spirit? Is it encouraging or negative? Does it build me up, make me feel empowered or does it accuse and condemn?" The Spirit encourages, affirms and never condemns. If we have sinned, the Spirit convicts, specifically with a way out – if it is from the enemy or our unhealed self, it is non-specific, grey, a fire blanket. The Spirit gives life: the enemy kills. The believer is never condemned, never hell bound. Condemnation and guilt turn us away from God. Holy Spirit conviction is Jesus saying, *"Come near to Me and away from your sin."*

Striving

Brennan Manning tells the story of an Irish priest who, whilst walking round his parish, sees an old peasant kneeling by the side of the road praying. Impressed, the priest says to the man, "You must be very close to God." The peasant looks up, thinks for a moment, smiles and says, "Yes, He's very fond of me."[34]

Often, we think it is about how we pray and listen, as though there is a merit award for hard work or a secret formula, if only we could find it. We think that listening to God is primarily about plans, purpose or answers to prayer. Underneath it all we want a special place with God, to be the good pupil who gets the gold star, turning good spiritual teaching to its own advantage. For example, I was always looking for answers, looking to unlock something. I missed the point – the answers are God Himself, not what I wanted God to provide.

I started to pray when I was eleven years old. I come from a completely non-Christian background, a family of shopkeepers and self-made businessmen, so I had absorbed an environment where the script was bargaining.

After becoming a Christian, my bargaining became more subtle, but God is not like a computer! If we are continually trying to find the right prayers to get the right answers we are kept in a place of perpetual unrest. It's no surprise that these demanding prayers go unanswered. Then the legalistic voice inside begins to say, "God is ignoring your prayers because you're not good enough." If we're eager or desperate enough to pursue prayer we intensify our efforts toward God. We work hard to find the 'correct method' to persuade God, constantly searching for new formulae for prayer. We get excited over new and better techniques, gadgets or systems to increase the effectiveness of our prayers.

We talk about 'believing in prayer', indicating how much we put our faith in our prayers and their power. This can lead to focusing on our own faith rather than God. Jesus tells the disciples that they can say to a mountain, *"Be cast into the sea!"* He began by saying, *"You must have faith in God."* (Mark 11:23) Whilst Matthew writes of Jesus teaching, *"If you have faith like a mustard seed, you can say to this mountain, 'move'."* (Chapter 17:20). So often I hear people saying, "I am not sure I have enough faith," as though our faith needs to be as big as the mountain (the word 'mountain' can symbolise troubles or problems). When we put our faith in God, small as it may be, we put our mustard seed in the centre of the mountain and look up to God, to the God who sees the mountain as a molehill! And as we look to Him, the Holy Spirit waters our seed, the warmth of God's love grows our seed and finally it breaks through the hard rock of the mountain.

We had a beautiful rose tree in the front garden opposite our house. The new occupants built a patio over the original garden for their cars. After a few years a new, very small, rose bush broke through the paving stones. A theophany moment – a little seed of faith, a mustard seed, can break through the mountain just like the seed from the almost destroyed rose tree can break through the patio.

However, when we are striving, we can believe that if we hear enough Bible facts or inspirational sermons 'it' is all bound to change. And if that doesn't work, we reinvent ourselves with Christian self-help books. This is worldly striving to 'get there' to get results, with a Christian veneer. It certainly isn't resting in the presence of Jesus. All the time we are making all this self-effort, trying to get ourselves right, we are deafened to the voice saying, "Let Me love you." We cannot hear the 'love lullaby'.

Sin

I do not believe sin separates us from the love of God, but I do believe it affects our communication. In "Sorry Matters", I have written a lot about confession and forgiveness – the two great gifts that enable us to be set free from sin. Here I just want to emphasise how it is a barrier to hearing God. Psalm 40:11-12, *"Do not withhold your mercy from me, O Lord …… my sins have overtaken me and I cannot see."* In The

Message it reads, *"When troubles ganged up on me, a mob of sins past counting, I was so swamped by guilt I couldn't see my way clear."* Sin blinds us. We need God's mercy and forgiveness so that we can see clearly. A way of describing how sin can be a barrier is to think about how we can have bad reception on a mobile phone. We were staying in a lovely thick-walled, stone cottage in Somerset which was wonderful. However, every time we wanted to make a telephone call we had to leave the cottage and when we were in the cottage we couldn't receive any calls. We didn't know if anyone was trying to make contact; we couldn't hear. This is what sin can do. We have to 'leave' the sin to get clear connection.

Worry and fear

I have written about some of the causes of worry and fear in "Mother Matters". Here, I just want to concentrate on how it is a barrier to hearing God. This was clearly highlighted to me in an experience I had during prayer. At the time, my meeting place with Jesus was a garden bench. I was using a way of prayer and meditation I had learned from Brad Jersak's book, "Can You Hear Me? Tuning in to the God Who Speaks". But on this particular morning, when I went to the bench, Jesus wasn't there. I found Him on the edge of a cliff. I said, "It's very near the edge." Jesus said, "Sometimes we have to leave the safety and tranquillity of the garden, but you are safe because I am with you." I said, "What do you want to talk about, Jesus?" He said, "We must step back from here for you to hear Me because the wind and the noise of the sea take my words away. Now you hear Me. That is what fear and worrisome emotions do – they take away my words. You need to step back to hear me and know I am with you when you cannot hear me."

Fear is much the same. It can completely overwhelm us. Many of us will have experienced not being able to remember something we know, such as when taking an exam, or if performing in public we get stage fright, when we 'forget' our lines or have them 'stolen' from us through fear. Fear robs us of our peace, our rest, our hope for a future and our believing that God has good plans for us. Fear can rob us of our ability to trust others and to receive love, tempting us to live in a fortress. Fear causes us to believe the lie that Satan has more power than He who is within us. The enemy encourages us to focus on the fear rather than on God. The enemy understands that once we start to focus on God, deliberately turning our minds away from the fear, and starting to praise and worship God, the fear will weaken. Then, once we get breakthrough and hear God's strengthening, comforting words, the fear disappears.

Materialistic awareness

I am using the word 'materialistic' not to denote consumerism, but the belief that what we experience through our five senses is more real than the presence of Jesus. Any pictures/visions are, if not dismissed, viewed as some sort of, maybe even divine, figment of the imagination rather than as revelation of the unseen reality of heaven here on earth. Remember in John 20:19, when the disciples were hiding behind locked doors, Jesus walked through the door; not because He was a ghost but because He had more substance than the door, much like when an aeroplane flies through a cloud and leaves the cloud still in one piece afterwards. The plane has more density than the cloud, just as when we are walking through mist, we are more solid.

The very first time I saw angels I was walking through the conference room at Swanwick Conference Centre. I saw several angels sitting on the rafters dangling their legs. I thought that can't be right, that is my imagination playing tricks; that's not what angels do!? As a team, we were gathering for prayer and William Barclay, who was Leanne Payne's pastor at the time, walked in and said, "Did anyone else see those angels sitting on the rafters?" We can't have both imagined it. God has graciously opened my eyes on many other occasions to angels and they usually look different. We need to ask God to tune the eyes and ears of our hearts to seeing these visitations. My car radio is set up so that, whatever I am listening to, the traffic news can cut in over the top. We need to pray our hearts are like that: whatever we are doing they are tuned in to God.

Limiting how God speaks

Finally, I hope we are no longer bound by the phrase, 'God spoke to Elijah in a still, small voice', as being the only way God speaks. This was very much emphasised to me when I first became a Christian and I can remember thinking, "If that is the only way God speaks, I will never hear Him!" So, as I have written, I asked God to speak in a loud voice to make things clear to me. And He did! The scripture this small voice quote comes from is 1 Kings 19:11-13, where a wind comes but God was not in the wind, then an earthquake, but God was not in the earthquake, then a fire and finally a whisper.

Contrast this with David in Psalm 29:3-9: *"The voice of the Lord is over the waters, the God of glory thunders, the Lord thunders over the mighty waters. The voice of the Lord is powerful, the voice of the Lord is majestic. The voice of the Lord breaks the cedars, the Lord breaks in pieces the cedars of Lebanon. He makes Lebanon skip like a calf. Sirion like a young wild ox. The voice of the Lord strikes with flashes of lightning. The voice of the Lord shakes the desert, the Lord shakes the Desert of Kadesh. The voice of the Lord twists the oaks and strips the forests bare. And in his temple all cry, 'Glory!'"*

Elijah found that Yahweh was not in the earthquake, wind, or fire, but in the silence. This stunning event stands in direct contrast to the experience of Moses on Mount Sinai. Moses experienced 'divine fireworks' and Elijah experienced 'sheer silence' but both experienced God. This is a vital teaching for us about the 'with-God' life. God may come to us in the dramatic and the spectacular or in the hidden and the ordinary. However and whenever and wherever God comes, we are to hear and obey.

The following are two stories that illustrate how God works when we listen:

Jean, a friend of mine, writes that a couple of friends who had been living in the Woodford area moved to Cornwall to look after elderly parents. When their parents died, they then decided to move back to Woodford, so they came up for a visit and to have a look around the area, but their main concern was the sale of their house in Cornwall. While they were visiting Jean, we sat down to pray together and I had a picture of two hands performing the children's game where you say, "Here is the church, here is the steeple, open the doors and see all the people." (I expect you know the rhyme and probably had it shown to you when you were little). My friends thought that maybe God was going to show them the church they would go to before he showed them the house. Anyway, we said our 'goodbyes', they said they would keep in touch and left. A couple of Sundays ago they both turned up at my church's evening service, having sold their house in Cornwall, and now looking for a new place to live! What they had to tell me really blew me away. Apparently, a family had come to look at the house – a couple, their son (who had autism) and the grandad. There is a church opposite the house with a clock that chimes the hour and the quarter hours. It struck while the family were looking round and the grandad put his hands together and said to the child, "Here is the church, here is the steeple, open the doors and see all the people."

Our friends were amazed and looked at each other and said, "That was Jean's word!" The couple decided to put in an offer on the house which, of course, was accepted and everyone thought the sale was settled. But a few days later the lady asked to come back to the house because she was worried that her little boy would be disturbed by the clock's chimes, especially at night-time, so perhaps it would be better for them not to have the house. The friends' hearts sank, but then one of them had the bright idea of persuading the lady to go up to the room where the boy would sleep to listen to the next chimes. While she was up there they both prayed and waited. When she came down she said, "I couldn't hear a thing!" The family are now living in the house and, hopefully, all is well.

The second story is from some other friends, Stuart and Ceri, who received some money from a family inheritance:

"We asked God what to do with it. He said, 'Put it to work.' Then we asked if we could look at a holiday home. He said, 'Go look.' We did some research and were drawn to Wales, due to family connections and price range. We travelled to Wales and as we crossed the border we listened to God and heard that we would buy something connected to revival history! As we rounded the next corner, we went under a rainbow and started laughing. We found nothing the first day (we had a miserable day and evening, but we knew to persevere). The next morning we asked God where we should look and both of us heard the name of a specific town we had never visited. We looked on the RightMove website on the internet and saw a non-conformist revival chapel called 'Chapel Ebenezer' recently drastically reduced! We put in an offer and had it accepted! When we walked in, we sensed the angels say, 'At last, people of faith!'"

WHOSE VOICE ARE YOU LISTENING TO?

Proverbs 4:20-27 (MSG): *"Dear friend, listen well to my words; tune your ears to my voice. Keep my message in plain view at all times. Concentrate! Learn it by heart! Those who discover these words live, really live; body and soul, they're bursting with health. Keep vigilant, watch over your heart; that's where life starts. Don't talk out of both sides of your mouth; avoid careless banter, white lies, and gossip. Keep your eyes straight ahead; ignore all sideshow distractions. Watch your step, and the road will stretch out smooth before you. Look neither right nor left; leave evil in the dust."*

Whilst talking to God once about my day, I wrote in my journal God's words to me: "I want a listening community. To have Me at the centre, both individually and corporately means to listen to Me; to listen to My love words, My encouragement; My desire is to be with you and spend time with you. When you don't know how much I love you, you are unable to believe this. I am never far from you but some of you need to turn your ear towards Me. Let Me love you."

Our difficulty is that God is not the only one whose voice we hear. The other voices are those of the world, the flesh and the devil.[35] We need to learn to discern the difference and to create a climate/atmosphere whereby it becomes easier to hear God's voice. The connection between the material and spiritual world is so strong that it affects everything. Every godly thought we have somehow taps into His blessings. Everything else is open to the enemy. For instance, negative, despairing thinking and words are dangerous because they are anti-hope and God is the God of hope. When we find ourselves thinking or speaking in this way, we need to confess it and ask for the blood of Jesus to cleanse and protect us.

Jesus tells us to be careful what we listen to.

Mark 4:24 (NLT): *"And be sure to pay attention to what you hear. The more you do this, the more you will understand – and even more, besides."*

"Listen carefully to what I am saying – and be wary of the shrewd advice that tells you how to get ahead in the world on your own." (MSG)

Who we listen to influences our beliefs and values and, therefore, those familiar voices affect our personal environment. If we like listening to negative views and moaning, we will attract people who like to criticise. Often in church people will say to me, "Have you heard...?" and I say, "Probably not," because people who want to gossip or moan know I won't give them much listening space! We set a standard for our ears by choosing to listen to God's voice more than any other, and by blocking or filtering those words which are not Kingdom words. The standard we set for our ears will then start to attract others who speak from a Kingdom/heavenly perspective. This gets easier over time.

Of course, we still meet with those who don't know Jesus, and we are seeking to influence them, but these are not friendships whose values we open ourselves up to. We need to develop deep friendships with people of faith. Such people display hope, promise, joy and encouragement. When we are vulnerable, we need to make sure that we are not with people who speak from a place of negativity or unbelief. *We* are responsible for the climate or environment we create – clear airways, a 'thin place'. If you plant two identical plants in different places in the garden and water and feed them the same but put one in the light and the other overlooked by other plants, you will find the one with space and light to grow will flourish. We are no different.

We need to surround ourselves with spiritually healthy people who speak 'God-life' and give us space to belong and grow. Spend time with other 'kings', 'priests' and members of God's army. Listen to our joint family history. If we don't know where we come from, we won't know where we are going or how to get there! Like the Old Testament prayers that begin with a history lesson to promote faith, we need people who can tell a God story. This doesn't mean we spend all our time in prayer meetings; it means we surround ourselves with people who encourage each other, enjoy each other, people we can relax with and laugh with, telling funny stories and recounting hilarious experiences – laughter really is good for the soul.

The voice of the world

When listening to God and seeking His rest, part of our confusion can be that the Bible presents the world in both a positive and negative light.

1 John 2:15-17 (MSG): *"Don't love the world's way. Don't love the world's goods. Love of the world squeezes out love for the Father. Practically everything that goes on in the world – wanting your own way, wanting everything for*

yourself, wanting to appear important – has nothing to do with the Father. It just isolates you from him. The world and all its wanting, wanting, wanting is on the way out – but whoever does what God wants is set for eternity."

God is the Creator of the world and rules the universe. He owns it, which is why we address Him as 'Lord'. The whole earth is full of God's glory (Isaiah 6:3). It is the world where God chose, through Jesus, to live among us. It is where the Holy Spirit is still active, within and through us. We have looked at how God speaks to us through His creation and reveals Himself through our everyday, ordinary encounters. All of creation was originally good; yet is now imperfect because of the entrance of sin and its effects on creation.

God's kingdom is different. God's world has a culture that is not of His Kingdom. The world's culture is what we have to learn to recognize and not be absorbed or shaped by. The culture of the world around us is selfish and fallen. It is full of ideas that seductively appeal to our fallen, selfish, false self, what the Bible calls our flesh. That is why visual advertising works. It appeals to the part of our brain that controls our emotions.

Paraphrasing from The Message, Romans 12:2 tells us not to be so well adjusted to our culture that we will be dragged down to its level of immaturity. James 4:4 warns us not to flirt with the world, while Colossians 2:8-10 (MSG) reads: *"Watch out for people who try to dazzle you with big words and intellectual double-talk. They want to drag you off into endless arguments that never amount to anything. They spread their ideas through the empty traditions of human beings and the empty superstitions of spirit beings. But that's not the way of Christ. Everything of God gets expressed in him so you can see and hear him clearly. You don't need a telescope, a microscope or a horoscope to realize the fullness of Christ, and the emptiness of the universe without Him. When you come to Him, that fulness comes together for you, too. His power extends over everything."*

As the Colossians verses state, we can be seduced by intellectual double-talk, and this applies especially if we feel less well educated. The world has a voice of secularised wisdom which may sound authoritative. Fear often causes us to listen to the wrong advice. We are vulnerable to treating perverted logic or dubious information as factual because we do not trust our God given abilities to discern God's truth.

In Numbers 13:1, God tells Moses to send spies into the promised land which He is going to give them. In Numbers 13:27-28, we read how two spies, Caleb and Joshua, came back saying, "It's fine, with the Lord's help we can take the land." But ten said, "No, there are giants in there." The children of Israel murmured and moaned, believed the negative reports and didn't go in. They did not trust what God had promised.

The story of David going to slay Goliath contains two very good illustrations on how not to be distracted by worldly wisdom. When David arrives at the camp where the battle with Goliath is about to take place, his brothers ask, "What are you doing here? Mind your own business! Go back to looking after your scrawny sheep!" David did not listen to his brothers. We also need to learn to not listen to those who seem to diminish us; those who joke in a sarcastic or aggressive way.

Proverbs 26:18-19 (MSG): *"People who shrug off deliberate deceptions, saying, 'I didn't mean it, I was only joking' are worse than careless campers who walk away from smouldering campfires."*

This may be passive anger, framed as a joke in case someone challenges it. If you speak out, the person can accuse you of not having a sense of humour or of being too sensitive. Remember, not all ungodly counsel comes from the ungodly. People in the Church can speak in ungodly language. We don't listen to a voice which seeks to control, is very dominant, critical or indeed, prescriptive – "This is what you should do", "This is the only way to do it". We must not act on the advice of someone who has their own agenda.

David won his first battle by not listening to his brothers. David knew God was greater than Goliath. Rumours of what David was saying reached King Saul, who sent for him. He tells Saul he believes he can kill the giant but Saul protests, "You're too young and inexperienced. I, Saul, have been in this fighting business before you were born!" David protests. His second battle is won as Saul says, "Go, and God help you."

This is a difficult battle to stand firm in. We can be put off, influenced by others' experience and their opinions that we are too young, not ready, not properly trained, not a professional soldier. Saul tries to make David a soldier by giving David his armour, a benevolent, well-intentioned gesture, but Saul's armour doesn't fit. Battle three is won when David refuses the armour.

Well-intentioned advice, when we sense it is not what God is saying to us, is very difficult to refute. It makes us feel bad and ungrateful. Although not godly, such words are not necessarily evil. They may be selfish but are usually motivated by fear; a desire to fix it for someone or to protect them, but the voice is ultimately a controlling one. I believe the enemy can only inflame any word that is not a Kingdom word. Think what would have happened if David had listened to any of those words.

As Proverbs 18:21 says, *"The tongue has the power of life or death."* In The Message, Proverbs 18:20-21 reads, *"Words satisfy the mind as much as fruit does the stomach; good talk is as gratifying as a good harvest. Words kill; words give life. They are either poison or fruit – you choose."*

We can choose to walk away from a conversation which leaves a 'bad taste' in our mouths. Our words are powerful: those we speak and those we listen to. A master orator and writer, Sir Winston Churchill knew the power of words. Martin Gilbert, Churchill's official biographer, wrote a book called "Churchill: The Power of Words". Churchill's words sing in a way that English language leaders and politicians have tried unsuccessfully to match ever since. Nevertheless, for all of us, words are powerful. With kind and encouraging words we can change a person's day – or even their entire life. My view of myself was completely changed when someone encouraged me by saying I was creative.

Your words have the power to bring great blessing. Look at Proverbs 10:11 (MSG): *"The mouth of the good person is a deep, life-giving well, but the mouth of the wicked is a dark cave of abuse."* Or a curse. Words have the power to destroy relationships. Hatred starts fights but *"Love pulls a quilt over the bickering,"* (Proverbs 10:12 MSG). Control of the tongue is vital. *"Too much talk leads to sin. Be sensible and keep your mouth shut,"* (Proverbs 10:19 NLT). Abraham Lincoln said, *"It is better to be silent and thought a fool than to speak and remove all doubt!"* Throughout this passage the writer of Proverbs contrasts 'the mouth of a fool' with 'the mouth of the righteous'. One speaks words of hatred; the other speaks words of love and wisdom. Words of hatred lead to violence, dissension, ruin and spreading slander. Words of love are a fountain of life; they cover over all wrongs. If someone has offended you, don't return the offence. Instead, return hatred with love. Speak well of the other.

I was in a room once when I saw in the Spirit a weird-looking creature flying around. It was a tongue with a pair of scissors on the end of it or, to put it another way, a pair of flying scissors made of tongue material! Later, during the week, I heard one of our team describing a host leader as 'someone with a sharp tongue', someone who used 'cutting words' or liked to 'cut people down to size with his tongue'. Psalm 64:3 (NLT) reads, *"They sharpen their tongues like swords and aim their bitter words like arrows."* People often say, "It just came out of my mouth. I didn't mean to say it," usually followed by, "You know what I'm like." James 3:8 says, *"But no man can tame the tongue."* It needs more than self-control because it is a symptom of something deeper. The Message goes on to say:

"This is scary: you can tame a tiger but you can't tame a tongue – it's never been done. The tongue runs wild, a wanton killer. With our tongues we bless God our Father; with the same tongues we curse the very men and women He made in His image. Curses and blessings out of the same mouth! My friends, this can't go on. A spring doesn't gush fresh water one day and brackish the next, does it? Apple trees don't bear strawberries, do they? Raspberry bushes don't bear apples, do they? You're not going to dip into a polluted mud hole and get a cup of clear, cool water, are you?"

James 1:19-21 paraphrase: "Lead with your ears, follow up with your tongue. In simple humility let our Gardener God landscape you."

Ungodly words are not necessarily evil. They may be selfish, sarcastic or controlling, usually, as I've said, because they are spoken out of fear. So, let's identify some of the unhelpful voices spoken to us by others, both in our current situations and past influences and voices. Remember that, although someone is dead, their voice can live on in our head for good or bad.

The voice of exaggeration

This is always dramatic language, "It's a disaster"; "This is the worst thing that has ever happened"; "It's left us all devastated"; "We (or the church, economy or the country) will never recover". This creates fear in us, or a negative view of life. Listen to what God says.

Or the exaggeration can be on the positive side but with a sting in the tail. "Oh, it was amazing, the best thing I have ever seen – I can't imagine anything could ever compare. Of course, such a shame you couldn't be there." This creates 'FOMO' (fear of missing out) and envy. Listen to God. *"They are without pity. Listen to their boasting. Their hearts are as hard as nails, their mouths blast hot air."* Psalm 17:10 (MSG)

The controlling, critical voice

We shouldn't listen to a voice which seeks to control; a voice which is dominating, critical or prescriptive, especially when the person has their own agenda. If we have had a very dominant parent, we often get used to being told what to do, or we believe all the critical words that have been spoken over us. This is not God's voice. These voices diminish us and cause us to doubt our own thoughts. God encourages us to become all He wants.

"I, yes I, am the one who comforts you. So why are you afraid of mere humans, who wither like the grass and disappear? Yet have you forgotten the Lord, Your Creator, the one who put the stars in the sky and established the earth? Will you remain in constant dread of human oppression? Will you continue to fear the anger of your enemies?" Isaiah 51:12-13 (NLT)

The negative, fearful voice

A voice that undermines our faith. Once fearful, 'survival' questions become the guiding questions of our lives, we start to stifle or dismiss God's words to us spoken from the 'house of love', illustrated by the children of Israel listening to the ten spies. So often God's words can sound unrealistic, sentimental, pious or useless. We may say, "I think God is saying..." This can be met with voices that say, "Yes, yes that sounds beautiful but..." The 'but' reveals how much we all can live in the grip of the world, a world that causes others to suggest we are naïve and need to be more realistic. In some groups, this 'realistic' approach can also undermine or diminish our enthusiastic faith. Sometimes in reviewing a meeting or conference with others, I start to wonder if I had been at the same meeting! I call this 'the drag factor'. Instead of focusing on all that God has done, the conversation becomes focused on what went wrong or didn't really work.

The flattering voice

To flatter means to pay someone a compliment or to over-praise someone, usually for gain or advantage. One morning at a conference I woke feeling odd – disturbed – and I asked God what the matter was. Into my mind came Psalm 62:4 (I did not know what it said): *"They are so friendly to my face while cursing me in their hearts."* (TLB) The antidote to this is the truth; Psalm 109:28 (NLT): *"Then let them curse me if they like but You will bless me."*

Learning not to trust everything said is quite difficult for us and feels wrong. We are told not to judge, but the Holy Spirit can alert us to others' 'hearts' wrongdoings. In John 2:24-25, these verses follow Jesus clearing the temple. It says that many believed Jesus because of His miraculous signs, *"But Jesus didn't trust them because He knew all about people. No-one needed to tell Him about human nature for he knew what was in each person's heart."* (NLT) These are challenging verses, when we read 1 Corinthians 13:7, "Love always trusts". But we need the Holy Spirit's wisdom and revelation in our relationships. We are not meant to be defensive and suspicious, so we need to balance what is being said with wisdom, and the grace-filled understanding, that none of us is perfect. We are all damaged, injured, flawed human beings and we may have deep, unacknowledged mixed motives. Whatever voices we are listening to that are not from God, imprison us and stop us from entering our place of rest.

The voice of negative self-talk

Even when I don't listen to those who are negative, controlling or diminishing, I sometimes still have to struggle with my own internal voices. If we have damaged hearts through the wounds we have received in childhood, they will be damaged further if we believe lies about ourselves. As children we are unable to sort out what is happening to us. We believe our parents to be right, so if we have been belittled, hurt, criticised or abused we think it must be our fault. So years later we listen to the critical, accusing, harsh words and believe them, or those from the scoffer and those who show us contempt. The voice inside whispers, "I am stupid, lazy, will never amount to anything."

This voice says, "I am no good, others are better than me, I will never make anything of my life, no-one loves me, no-one understands me." We listen to those lies and, because they are familiar, they are comfortable. We often prefer these to the voice of love that bids, "Come, follow Me." Or when we are unable to accept God's voice (because we don't believe we are good enough) we put ourselves on a self-improvement programme or endeavour to do everything 'correctly'.

The voice of the flesh

In Christian theology the world, the flesh and the devil are often described as sources of temptation as they are considered in opposition to the Trinity. We can see these roots in the parable of the sower; the devil (birds eating the seed), weak flesh (shallow and unreceptive believers) and the world (cares of this life and the lure of wealth). It is a metaphor to describe sinful tendencies. Galatians 2:20 in The Message reads, *"I identified myself completely with Him. Indeed, I have been crucified with Christ. My ego is no longer central. It is no longer important that I appear righteous before you or have your good opinion, and I am no longer driven to impress God."* Dying to ego equals no striving – rest. This 'flesh voice' is opposed to the Spirit both in wanting to drag us down and in falsely elevating us.

The voice of despair

This voice has unholy alliances with shame, negativity and lack of self-acceptance. This voice says, for example, "God doesn't do anything for me. He never speaks to me. He can do anything but not for me. What's the point of talking to Him? He never answers me. He does things for everyone else but not for me."

We can allow circumstances to cause us to despair, continually wanting life to be different. In Genesis 39:3, it says that God was with Joseph in a special way. Joseph was in Potiphar's house and, although at this time he was experiencing favour, it was still in Egypt; still not where he would like to have been.

We can often think, because our circumstances are bad – or not as we think they should be – God is not with us. Despair refuses to accept God's grace in the present moment and we resent any idea of accepting and resting where we are; a dismal place of misunderstanding rather than a place to encounter the Father heart of God. Martyn Lloyd Jones said, *"Stop listening to yourself and start talking to yourself!"* by which he meant, "Turn off the negative voice and start speaking (out loud if you can) God's truths". There are a number of people I see who believe that God can do almost anything for anyone else, but not for them. That is the flesh. That is our unhealed self talking to us, cancelling out, monitoring. This despairing part of our mind can quench the life of the Spirit in us. It has a companion.

The voice of law

When I first became a Christian I could not understand how the Pharisees failed to see Jesus as the Son of God. The longer I have been a Christian, the more I have wondered if I would have recognised Him, because we can easily build up a prejudiced, religious view of what is or is not acceptable. This is a Pharisaical voice, clinging to the Law. Quoting Michael L Brown, *"Legalism is … laws without love, rules without relationship and standards without a Saviour."* The gospel is transformation from the inside out. Religion is rules from outside. I prayed, "Dear Jesus, I am not sure I always recognise Pharisaical behaviour. I think maybe I can be one myself." God answered me, "Clinging to relationship rather than knowledge is always difficult, but just continue to come and talk to me every day. Being wrong or right doesn't worry me as much as it does you."

The grandiose voice

Because of the complexities of the heart, we can listen to a very self-abasing voice and then switch to a self-seeking, self-promoting voice of presumption. This voice comes from the part of our ego that tempts us into empty fantasies, the grandiose unrealistic expectation. When spiritualised, this sounds like the voice of victorious living. But it is victory with limited commitment, a belief system that the Christian life 'lived properly' is without struggle, wilderness experiences or trials. Leon D Thomassian speaks of 'the crown without the cross'.[36] False prophecies often fuel our fantasies of self-importance, causing us to be dissatisfied with our lives together with an ungodly striving. Not very restful!

It can be a very romantic, deceptive voice. (There was a young single curate of a large London church. At least two women said to me that God had told them he would be their husband!) Or it can be a voice that tempts us with promises of money, power or fame. Our difficulty is that these aims or goals are not necessarily wrong in themselves but can subtly take us off course when we justify them with a spiritual spin. They can so easily enslave us, causing us to pursue something that is not Jesus' 'easy yoke'.

Money isn't wrong. We need it. It is our love of money that's the issue. In a Godly project or ministry, it can be so easy to become focused on how to raise money, or on how to find sponsors or supporters, that we subtly stop trusting God as our provider. Fundraising can end up creating restless anxiety no matter how good the cause. We need to learn to listen to the voice that says, "Trust me." Our response needs to be, "I submit this plan to You. If it is Your plan, You will bless it; show me any action I need to take." Money is 'daily manna', daily bread, and we find this hard.

When my husband died, one of the voices I had to fight not to listen to was 'not enough'. The pensions were halved, and I couldn't imagine how I could continue with the same lifestyle in the same house that I was not ready to leave. Yes, I did have to make some changes and cancel some standing orders and direct debits, but at the end of that first year I still had the same amount of money in the bank as at the beginning of the year. That voice, however, still tempts me when I look to the future, the fearful thought being, "I will run out, there will not be enough."

There is also the voice of the desire for power. This deception starts the minute we change the word 'power' to 'influence'. Yes, of course, we need to influence for good and extend God's Kingdom by telling others about Jesus, but when that voice combines with the voice of the desire for fame it can be toxic. The voice of power tempts us to captivate others and to have control over them, no matter how benevolent our intention. The voice of fame enslaves us in empty fantasy and a continuous desire for others' admiration. We try to gain popularity by performance. These voices are all self-seeking, self-centred and wanting to please ourselves rather than God. It is not a restful place.

The voice of the devil

This voice uses a different pronoun. It does not say, "I am stupid," it says, "*You* are stupid." Most spiritual warfare takes place in our minds with the devil questioning, "Did God really say…?" and all other condemning words. The Bible teaches us that Satan is the accuser of the brethren. As I have written elsewhere, Satan's lies imprison us as he is the 'father of lies'. Jesus comes to set the prisoners free and the Holy Spirit leads us into truth. The great battles in our minds are between lies and truth. Unfortunately, we often cooperate with Satan by recycling his lies.

We may or may not cooperate with him in terms of accusing other people, but we are very good at accusing ourselves. The powers of darkness simply turn up the volume on the unhealed 'tapes' in our heads and leave us to it. They only have to start the first sentence, for example. We are so familiar with the voice that it feels like truth, so we agree with all self-accusation and self-condemnation. That is not the Holy Spirit speaking to us. That is NOT God's voice to us. We need not only to hear God's voice but, in order to *know* God's voice, we also need to know what He is saying in some of our unhealed areas so that we can be defined by Him. God does not see us as we see ourselves – so agree with Him!

When we have a sinful reaction to a wound – such as self-hatred, as a result of shame and rejection – the enemy is able to sow seeds of lies. When someone has sinned against us, and we continue to nurse unforgiveness, bitterness and the desire for revenge, the enemy will inflame these dark thoughts/voices. The enemy tests us by attempting to divide us from our brothers and sisters in Christ and causes us to doubt our value to God; we do not believe we have continuous oneness with our heavenly Father.

One of this voice's most successful deceptions is to convince us that we have not done enough; we have not prayed enough, read our Bible enough and things have gone wrong, or not happened, because of our failure to be 'enough'. This leads to an anxious worrying spiritual response. Often the root wound is our inability to trust God. We need to ask the Holy Spirit to reveal our wound so that we can ask Jesus to heal it and bring captive the lies that the wound has caused us to believe.

HOW TO LISTEN WELL

We need to listen with both sides of our mind, left hemisphere (head) which is word based, and right hemisphere (heart) which is symbol based. So to begin, let's look at listening to the word.

Listening through scripture

Psalm 74:9-10 (ESV): *"We do not see our signs. There is no longer any prophet and there is none among us who knows how long. How long, Oh Lord, is the foe to scoff? Is the enemy to revile Thy name forever?"*

(MSG): *"There is not a sign or symbol of God in sight, nor anyone to speak in His Name, no-one knows what is going on."*

Quoting Elizabeth Goudge, from "The Scent of Water":
"They had no signs; little by little it had been stolen from them."

Using scripture as a signpost:

1. Take some promises, for example Matthew 28:20 (TPT): *"And teach them to faithfully follow all I have commanded you. And never forget I am with you every day, even to the completion of this age."* Meditate on them. Let them feed you so that they become that living word in you, a living stone that slays giants!

2. Respond with your needs, your fears and your giants.

3. Listen again for God's response to you.

Or:

1. Personalise Jesus' words – especially His instructions. Luke is a good gospel to use, especially if you have a Red Letter Bible.

2. Respond about your resistance, your reluctance, your excuses or your desire to 'say yes'.

3. Listen again for God's response to you.

4. Write out God's promises and, again, be honest in your response; include your doubts or fears.

God is too real to be anywhere else but in reality. Remember that God wants intimate relationships with us because He is our Father. He went looking for Adam in the Garden of Eden in the evening breeze, much like a Dad popping round to see us to find out what sort of day we have had. We would trust a good Dad enough to be honest. Denial and pretending puts us outside of God's reality.

Scripturally guided meditation

Another way of listening is a scripturally guided meditation using our true imagination.

From "My Utmost for His Highest", Oswald Chambers: "The people of God in Isaiah's day had starved their imagination by looking on the face of idols, and Isaiah made them look up at the heavens; that is, he made them begin to use their imagination aright. Nature to a saint is sacramental. If we are children of God, we have a tremendous treasure in Nature. In every wind that blows in every night and day of the year, in every sign of the sky, in every blossoming and in every withering of the earth, there is a real coming of God to us if we will simply use our starved imagination to realise it ... Is your imagination looking on the face of an idol? Is the idol yourself? Your work? ... Then your imagination of God is starved, and when you are up against difficulties you have no power, you can only endure in darkness ... Deliberately turn your imagination to God ... If you have been bringing every thought ... to Christ, it will be one of the greatest assets to faith when the time of trial comes, because your faith and the Spirit of God will work together. Learn to associate ideas worthy of God with all that happens in Nature – the sunrises and the sunsets, the sun and the stars, the changing seasons, and your imagination will never be at the mercy of your impulses (food, sex, pornography, what I fear, how I feel), but will be filled with images of glory ... Imagination is the greatest gift God has given us, and it ought to be devoted entirely to Him."

Do you remember at the beginning of this Chapter I wrote of Fred and his biblical meditations from "God of Surprises"? We are going to practice a different biblical story now.

Luke 8:40-48

This is the story of Jesus going to heal Jairus' daughter. On His way to Jairus' house, Jesus is stopped by a woman with a haemorrhage. Picture the scene in your mind. There is a crowd there; the disciples; a woman who is bleeding who should have been kept away; there is the father and there is the servant who comes from the father's house. You can choose to be any one of these people except Jesus. Just have a think now who you want to be before you read on. I am going to help you to imagine yourself there.

I want you to feel the warmth and to picture that blue, Middle Eastern sky. There is a lake and, probably, you are standing on gritty sand. On the side of the lake the crowd has received Jesus with open arms, for they have been waiting for Him, and now a man named Jairus – the leader of the Jewish synagogue – comes and falls down at Jesus' feet and begs Him to come with him for his only child is dying, a little girl of twelve years old. Jesus goes with him, pushing through the crowds.

As they are doing this, a woman who wants to be healed comes up behind and touches Him. She has been slowly bleeding for twelve years and can find no cure, though she has spent everything she had on doctors. At the instant she touches the edge of His robe, the bleeding stops. *"Who touched me?"* Jesus asks. Everyone denies it. Peter says, *"Master, so many are crowding against you."* But Jesus tells him, *"No, it was someone who deliberately touched me because I felt healing power go out from me."* When the woman realises Jesus knows, she begins to tremble and falls to her knees before Him and tells Him why she touched Him and that now she is well. *"Daughter,"* He says to her, *"Your faith has healed you! Go in peace."* While He is still speaking to her, a messenger arrives from Jairus' home with the news that the little girl is dead. "She has gone," he tells Jairus. "There is no use bringing the Teacher now." But when Jesus hears what has happened, He says to the father, *"Don't be afraid. Just trust Me and she will be alright."*

Try to stay here and not rush on to the known 'happy ending'.

Now, stay with your picture for a minute. Just acknowledge what is going on for you in the picture. Stay present with Jesus and yourself. I am going to ask you a few questions to help you look at yourself. Look, for instance, where you are in the crowd. Are you one of the crowd members? Or standing at the back as an observer? Or are you near Jesus? What happened with the woman when Jesus turned round? Did you look away or feel embarrassed? If you were the father of the daughter, did you feel anxious?

Let me tell you what happened to me when I first did this. I was, in fact, one of the disciples with Jesus and I was quite close to Him when we got out of the boat. When the father came up that was fine, and I was jostling through the crowd close to Jesus. When all this started to happen with the woman, I was thinking, "We have got to get to the house but now we have this delay." I was getting quite anxious. I then took my eyes completely off Jesus. I could see the servant coming from the house, could see from the look on his face that it was bad news, and I distanced myself. Whilst I had been quite close to all that was happening, I now thought "there is trouble coming," and I actually found myself stepping back two or three places into the crowd. I didn't run away, but I distanced myself. Now that was very much what God was speaking to me about at the time, because I don't like conflict. When I saw trouble coming, I basically distanced myself to see how the land was lying because it scared me. I would worry about what I perceived the conflict to be.

We can practice this way of listening with many of the bible stories, asking God to reveal to us that which needs healing and transforming in us.

Here is another example. I knew a young man who came to me for healing prayer who sat with a notebook and wrote down everything I said. One of his problems was that he felt he didn't belong in any group in the church. He had been fostered and had had a very broken life. I suggested between sessions that he did an imaginative meditation on the wedding at Cana, saying he could be anyone but Jesus. The next week he came back and said he had to gatecrash the wedding because he didn't have an invitation and had gone as the local village reporter. So we began to look at how he could be a guest and need not take a notebook with him.

Garden of the heart

This exercise is a way of listening to God with the right hemisphere part of our mind (heart). Think about your heart as a garden and ask God to show you the fruit (maybe branches needing to be pruned) or any doubts and fears (weeds needing to be pulled up). Ask Jesus to come as the Gardener.

Pray: Father, please come by the power of Your Holy Spirit and show me my garden. Protect me from unprofitable, destructive introspection and reveal to me my heart as You see it. We thank You, Father, that You are the Gardener.

Isaiah 58:11 (NLT): *"The Lord will guide you continually, giving you water when you are dry and restoring your strength. You will be like a well-watered garden, like an ever-*

flowing spring."

Read John 15 (The Vine). With Jesus, look for any weeds of fear/doubt. Name them, pull them up and see what Jesus does with them. Look for anything that needs pruning. Even good branches need pruning. Name it. Ask Jesus to help.
Look at the fruit – answered prayer, fruits of the Spirit, influence in others' lives. Look for any dried-up areas, where you have lost hope.

Song of Songs 4:12: *"You are a garden locked up, my sister, my bride; you are a spring enclosed, a sealed fountain."*

The very first time I did this exercise I was in Germany with Leanne Payne. It was the first time I had met her. When we did this exercise, I saw a very organised garden – a bit like a well-manicured park – but as I looked closer there was bindweed underneath all the flowers. I asked Jesus to help me to name the weed and it was 'fear of disapproval'. It was a small conference of about forty delegates and Leanne asked us to say what we saw. I related my experience to which she replied, "Ah yes, women in ministry often suffer from this." I knew it was true but left wondering how she knew I was in ministry as we had never met. I had been a Christian for about ten years and she was the first prophet I had met of this calibre.

Another time, whilst doing this exercise, Jesus led me to a desolate, dried-up part of my garden with a broken wishing well. Immediately I knew what it meant. I had been desperately praying for someone's healing and they had died. I understood that my prayers had no longer been focused on Father God but had developed into a mixture of striving and wishful thinking. I confessed all this. Then I saw water spring up in the corner of this forsaken area and soon everywhere was flooded and had become a luscious green area. There was no sight of the wishing well.

On another occasion I was wondering whether to see a couple of people who wanted prayer because they had a history of having been sexually abused. The garden of my heart revealed a large tree which Jesus was standing by. He was inviting me to sit with Him but all around the trunk of the tree were stinging nettles that He wanted me to pull up. I would have liked gardening gloves but had lace gloves. Somehow, gingerly and reluctantly, I started to pull them up and give them to Jesus. He took them from me and rubbed them into His chest, absorbing all the pain of the stinging nettles. Needless to write, I said yes to the requests.

I hope, by this point in the book, you are beginning to make the connection that to rest means to live without anxiety, and for me the only way I understand this is if I am able to listen to Father God's heartbeat, thereby walking with Jesus, sharing His yoke, and thereby experiencing the unforced rhythms of grace. I think Jesus walks slowly and He does not mind interruptions because, in this unhurried life, He has all the time it takes to listen well to others alongside listening to the Father. Only from the place of rest do we have time for others. The Western world's lifestyle has stolen our time.

LISTENING TO EACH OTHER

Isaiah 50:4 (TLB): *"The Lord God has given me His words of wisdom so that I may know what to say to all these weary ones. Morning by morning He wakens me and opens my understanding to His will."*

This was one of the first verses that leapt out at me when I became a Christian. I wrote in the margin of my Bible, "Do that for me." Nothing appealed to me more than hearing God and speaking His word to others.

Healthy listening to others

Eugene Peterson writes: *"We live in a noisy world. We are yelled at, promoted, called. Everyone has an urgent message for us. We are surrounded with noise; telephone, radio, television, stereo. Messages are amplified deafeningly. The world is a mob in which everyone is talking at once and no-one is willing or able to listen. But God listens. He not only speaks to us, but He also listens to us. His listening to us is an even greater marvel than His speaking to us. It is rare to find anyone who listens carefully and thoroughly. When it happens, we know that what we say and feel are immensely important. We acquire dignity. We never know how well we think or speak until we find someone who listens."*[37]

How do we start to listen well, so that the other person begins to feel important and blossom? We need to learn to be 'all ears'. It is said that good listening is not only listening to what the person says but hearing what they mean. When we looked at this in my Monday Group (a group of ladies who meet each week), the following were a few of the issues which made us feel the opposite to being heard well. These were not in respect of counselling; these were with regard to normal conversations.

Interrupting was the big one. We decided we interrupt or are interrupted when the listener is not interested, or busier thinking about what they want to say, for example "Yes, that's just like me," or "Yes, that is what … is like," etc. We also interrupt when we are a more factual person and the person talking is expressing feelings or ideas in a 'circular' way, maybe more intimate or self-revealing than we are comfortable with. As the person listening, we can just be lost because we do not know what they are talking about, so we interrupt or try to control the conversation.

Being task-orientated does not make for good listening. Early advice-giving is a killer to the feeling of being heard. I used to say to my husband, Ron, "I just want to tell you about this, I do not want you to tell me what to do!" I once advised one wife to try this with her husband. Unfortunately, he replied, "If you don't want my advice what's the point of telling me?" Not a good recipe for listening. When we feel heard, we feel loved and feel rested, at peace. Try to have some level of eye contact. Looking past the person to see what else is going on, or who else wants to talk to you, is not careful listening.

John Stott spoke of 'double listening', which is listening to the word and the world.[38] We cannot really listen well unless we can listen to God. Only from a place of rest can we hear others. We do not feel known if the person listening is too busy, even if it is in their head. Dietrich Bonhoeffer said, *"The first service that one owes to others in fellowship consists of listening to the Father's word, so the beginning of love for the brother is learning to listen to him."*[39] To paraphrase him, we so often think we must always contribute something when we are in the company of others, forgetting that listening can be a greater service than speaking. Henri Nouwen called listening 'the highest form of hospitality'.

From "Rules for a New Brother" by The Brakkenstein
Community of Blessed Sacrament Fathers:

Obedience also demands of you
That you listen to the other person
Not only to what he is saying
But to what he is
Then you will begin to live in such a way
That you neither crush nor dominate
Nor entangle your brother
But help him to be himself
And lead him to freedom.

Remember, never see the person as they see themselves.
Ask God for His view of the person. The following is a
wonderful example of learning to listen and not be deceived
by outward appearances.

Extract from "Abba's Child" by Brennan Manning

Once I related the story of an old man dying of cancer. The
old man's daughter had asked the local priest to come and
pray with her father. When the priest arrived, he found the
man lying in bed with his head propped up on two pillows
and an empty chair beside his bed. The priest assumed that
the old fellow had been informed of his visit.
"I guess you were expecting me?" he said.
"No, who are you?" (Old fellow)
"I'm the new associate at your parish," the priest replied.
"When I saw the empty chair, I figured you knew I was going
to show up."
"Oh yeah, the chair," said the bedridden man. *"Would you
mind closing the door?"*
Puzzled, the priest shut the door.

"I've never told anyone this, not even my daughter," said the man, *"but all my life I have never known how to pray. At the Sunday Mass I used to hear the pastor talk about prayer, but it always went right over my head. Finally, I said to him one day, in sheer frustration, "I get nothing out of your homilies on prayer."*

"Here," says my pastor, reaching into the bottom drawer of his desk. "Read this book by Hans Urs von Balthasar. He's a Swiss theologian. It's the best book on contemplative prayer in the twentieth century."

"Well, Father" says the man, "I took the book home and tried to read it but in the first three pages I had to look up twelve words in the dictionary. I gave the book back to my pastor, thanked him, and under my breath whispered, 'for nothin'. I abandoned any attempt at prayer," he continued, *"Until one day about four years ago my best friend said to me, 'Joe, prayer is just a simple matter of having a conversation with Jesus. Here's what I suggest. Sit down on a chair, place an empty chair in front of you and in faith see Jesus on the chair. It's not spooky because He promised, 'I'll be with you always.' Then just speak to Him and listen in the same way you're doing with me right now.'"*

"So, Padre, I tried it and I've liked it so much that I do it a couple of hours every day. I'm careful though. If my daughter saw me talking to an empty chair she'd either have a nervous breakdown or send me off the funny farm!"

The priest was deeply moved by the story and encouraged the old guy to continue on the journey. Then he prayed with him, anointed him with oil and returned to the rectory. Two nights later the daughter called to tell the priest that her Daddy had died that afternoon.

"Did he seem to die in peace?" he asked.

"Yes," she answered, *"When I left the house, around two o'clock, he called me over to his bedside, told me one of his corny jokes and kissed me on the cheek. When I got back*

from the store an hour later, I found him dead. But there was something strange, Father. In fact, beyond strange, kinda weird. Apparently just before Daddy died, he leaned over and rested his head on a chair beside his bed."

So to return to my central theme on rest, I want to look at John 13:23 (KJV): *"Now there was leaning on Jesus' bosom one of his disciples, whom Jesus loved."*

Firstly, we need to learn to not hurry past such verses. "To read verse twenty-three without faith is to read it without profit. To risk the passionate life, we must be 'affected by' Jesus, as John was. We must engage His experience with our lives rather than with our memories. Until I lay my head on Jesus' breast, listen to His heartbeat and personally appropriate the Christ experience of John's eyewitness, I have only a derivative spirituality. My cunning imposter will borrow John's moment of intimacy and attempt to convey it as if it were my own."[40]

We too can learn and listen. From this position of oneness in the Father's love, we listen to His rhythm. The fragmentation of my heart starts to mend. I am enfolded in love. We can listen to the heartbeat of God. I am rested.
Secondly, we need to understand how John describes himself, as the 'one Jesus loved'. He could have written, "I am an apostle and evangelist, the author of several well-known letters and one of the gospels."

How do we define ourselves? There is more about this in the following Chapter. Suffice to write here, as we come to really know ourselves, we are able to live in the 'unforced rhythms of grace' (Matthew 11:28, MSG) and live an anxious-free life, thereby being an anxious-less presence to others.

Chapter 4

IDENTITY

The preceding Chapter could be the end of the book but for the fact that there are other factors which rob us of our rest or block us from ever fully entering into the rest on offer. One of these 'rest robbers' is our lack of, or insecure, identity. God, who is the source of life, is also our foundation for living. If we do not have a sense of God being first as our foundation, we will never get life right; never get our lives in order so we can experience the gift of rest, the unforced rhythms of grace. God cannot be an optional extra, living on the margins of our life. It has to be God at the centre, first and last; Jesus, Alpha and Omega, and all of the letters in between; Jesus, the 'In the beginning', Word made flesh, become man; Jesus at the beginning before the foundation of the earth; the Trinity, the love relationship spilling over into making the world, making us! So the beginning of our story is before the creation of earth!

C S Lewis tells this well in the Narnia stories. He writes of the 'deeper magic from before the dawn of time.' In the story the witch tells Aslan that he has a traitor with him.

"Well," said Aslan. *"His offence was not against you."*
"Have you forgotten the Deep Magic?" asked the Witch.
"Let us say I have forgotten it," answered Aslan gravely.
"Tell us of this Deep Magic."
"Tell you?" said the Witch, her voice growing suddenly shriller. *"Tell you what is written on that very Table of Stone which stands beside us?" Tell you what is written in letters deep as a spear is long on the fire stones on the Secret Hill? Tell you what is engraved on the sceptre of the Emperor-*

beyond-the-Sea? You at least know the Magic which the Emperor put into Narnia at the very beginning. You know that every traitor belongs to me as my lawful prey and that for every treachery I have a right to a kill."

Then Aslan takes the place of Edmund (the traitor) and is sacrificed but returns to life and is greeted by the girls, Lucy and Susan.

"Oh, you're real, you're real! Oh, Aslan!" cried Lucy, and both girls flung themselves upon him and covered him with kisses.

"But what does it all mean?" asked Susan when they were somewhat calmer.

"It means," said Aslan, *"that though the Witch knew the Deep Magic, there is a magic deeper still which she did not know. Her knowledge goes back only to the dawn of time. But if she could have looked a little further back, into the stillness and the darkness before Time dawned, she would have read there a different incantation. She would have known that when a willing victim who had committed no treachery was killed in a traitor's stead, the Table would crack and Death itself would start working backwards."* [41]

So before the foundation of the earth, in a time before time, our rescue, our healing, our restoration and our forgiveness were already planned. 2 Timothy 1:9 (NRSV): *"... God, who saved us and called us with a holy calling, not according to our works but according to his own purpose and grace. This grace was given us in Christ Jesus before the ages began."*

1 Peter 1: 18-20 (NRSV): *"You know you were ransomed from the futile ways inherited from your ancestors, not with perishable things like silver or gold, but with the precious blood of Christ, like that of a lamb without defect and*

blemish. He was destined before the foundation of the world but revealed at the end of the ages for your sake."
In The Message, verse 20 reads, *"Even though it has only lately – at the end of the ages – become public knowledge, God has always known He was going to do this for you."*

1 Corinthians 2:6-10 (MSG): *"We, of course, have plenty of wisdom to pass on to you once you get your feet on firm spiritual ground, but it's not popular wisdom, the fashionable wisdom of high-priced experts that will be out-of-date in a year or so. God's wisdom is something mysterious that goes deep into the interior of his purposes. You don't find it lying around on the surface. It's not the latest message, but more like the oldest – what God determined as the way to bring out his best in us, long before we ever arrived on the scene. The experts of our day haven't a clue about what this eternal plan is. If they had, they wouldn't have killed the Master of the God-designed life on a cross. That's why we have this Scripture text: 'No-one's ever seen or heard anything like this. Never so much as imagined anything quite like it – What God has arranged for those who love him.' But you've seen and heard it because God by his Spirit has brought it all out into the open before you."*

And so we come to the creation story, with our rescue, healing and forgiveness woven into the tapestry of the beginning of the earth. But we are born into a world that has fallen, where trust in our Creator has died, been forgotten and we have lost connection.

Imagine: Once upon a time there was a tiny blob of being created by the King of Heaven and deep in this being was a stamp "M.I.H" – Made In Heaven – the blob's identity or ID was Imago Dei or, in English, Image of the Divine. However, this tiny blob of being was born into the Land of Doing. He/she slowly lost contact with his/her original creator and they became more and more conformed to the world and less and less their true selves/original being/original design, often deafened by the world, unable to hear the lullaby of the Father's love and blind to God's presence.

We see this story played out in stories and films. Fictional stories and films depict the same loss of identity and the journey taken to reconnect. For example, In the story of Superman, Clark Kent is sent from the planet Krypton and is found and adopted by the Kent family. Clark has a crystal which leads him to an ice field which, when he throws the crystal down, melts and reveals a huge crystalline building. This fortress contains memory crystals which enable him to make contact with Krypton. Clark visits the ice palace ('palace of solitude') where there is a statue of his parents. He visits to make connection with his true identity. David Crawley found this quote when we were thinking about Superman. It is at the point of the film where Superman is learning about his true identity and purpose.

"You will travel far, my little one, but we will never leave you. Even in the face of our death the richness of our lives shall be yours. All that I have, all I've learned, everything I feel, all this and more I bequeath you, my son. You will carry me inside you all the days of your life. You will make my strength your own and all my life through your eyes as your life will be seen through mine. The son becomes the father, the father becomes the son. This is all I can send you."

The story of Tarzan has a similar background story. His parents die and he is brought up by apes but finds his parents' home in the jungle, where he looks at photos, teaches himself to read and discovers his true identity.

Paraphrasing John Eldredge: "Earlier in the story, back in the beginning of our time on earth, a great glory was bestowed upon us. We all – men and women – were created in the image of God. Fearfully and wonderfully made, fashioned as living icons of the bravest, wisest, most stunning person who ever lived. Those who have ever seen him fell to their knees without even thinking about it, much like you find yourself stunned by the beauty of the Alps or a waterfall, dawn or sunset. That glory was shared with us. We were, as G K Chesterton says, 'statues of God walking about in a garden', endowed with strength and beauty all our own. All that we ever wished we could be we were and more."[42]

Irenaeus said, "The glory of God is a man fully alive."

Genesis 1:27 (MSG) *"He created them godlike."* (ESV) *"So God created man in his own image, in the image of God he created him; male and female he created them."*

So our original glory comes before the sin and is deeper to our nature. We were crowned with glory and honour. We fell and our glory faded. As we come into freedom, we recognise more and more the person God called us to be in His original masterpiece, His blueprint. Freedom means continually being or allowing ourselves to be 'unwrapped' from all the layers of fallenness that hide our beauty: the fear of God's disapproval, the fear of others' opinions, the false 'fig leaves' or coverings we make for ourselves because of this fear.[43] When we fell in the Garden, the beauty of God's image within us became marred/broken and we allowed Satan to steal our identity. We no longer knew who we were.

"Now God has us where He wants us, with all the time in this world and the next to shower grace and kindness upon us." Ephesians 2:7 (MSG).

We are always in the process of becoming. We find those parts of our lives that are working well, that we are pleased with and find acceptable, and when we find them or acknowledge them this gives us energy, confidence and assurance. We are affirmed. We are also always in the process of being corrected, refined and transformed. God's relentless pursuit of us insists that we face up to our sloth, our pride, our selfishness, our avarice – all the things that separate us from God's complete victory in us. We are also in the process of being motivated; the call upon our life to embrace living life to the full, abundantly, and this motivation and invitation, must sustain us through every shadowed valley and every parched wilderness.

Thus, we could say to be born in sin is to come into this world with a sin nature, our old nature. We are born partially covered in 'layers' of a false self that was never God's original intention. This original creation is the part that is going to live forever. The false self is the one that wants to live outside the radius of God's will and God's love, outside of reality, outside of our inheritance, outside of our 'being-life' (God as the source of all being), outside of eternal life. The false self is, to some extent, illusory and does not want to be or cannot be adopted into the family of God.

So the secret of my identity is in the love and mercy of God. Therefore I cannot hope to find myself anywhere except in Him. Ultimately, the only way I can be myself is to become identified with Jesus, in whom is hidden the reason and fulfilment of my existence. If I find Him, I will find myself and if I find my true self, I will find Him. C S Lewis said, *"You can't find yourself when looking for yourself; you find yourself when looking for Jesus."* We are both created by God and adopted by Him. He knows us, knew us before the foundation of the earth and comes looking for us, wanting to find and adopt us.

Adopted into God's family

Romans 8: 14-17 (NRSV): *"For all who are led by the Spirit of God are children of God. For you did not receive a spirit of slavery to fall back into fear, but you have received a spirit of adoption. When we cry 'Abba, Father', it is that very Spirit bearing witness with our spirit that we are children of God, and if children, then heirs, heirs of God and joint heirs with Christ – if, in fact, we suffer with him so we may also be glorified with him."*

When we are adopted into God's family, it is not as if we are adopted into some new family, but into the family we were always meant to be in. We arrive home. There was a story in the newspapers a few years ago of a missionary couple who found, having given birth, that their baby had been swapped. They kept the baby they had been given, but the parents went looking for the lost one, the one who bore their DNA, which they eventually found. Now, of course, we all carry something of God's 'DNA', His image in us, and He comes looking for us to bring us back home, to clean us up, restore us, heal us and bless us.

Part of our identity is understanding our adoption. We are born again into God's family, a royal family. Adoption is where we learn to reconnect with our true personhood, chosen, premeditated, planned. It is possible for someone to get pregnant by mistake, but no-one can adopt by mistake.

In biblical times, babies and children were not adopted. Coming of age, like a bar-mitzvah, was an illustration of adoption. Greek and Roman adoption happened around the age of 30, when someone was chosen to be the special one in the family.

In the time when Jesus lived, it was the Jewish custom that when a businessman or wealthy farmer felt his son was ready to become part of the family business, he would take him to the market square and declare publicly, "This is my beloved son, in whom I am well pleased." A beloved child, ready to join the family business. God does not want us to stay as infants. He wants us childlike, not childish, and in the 'family business'. Our destiny is from a Saturday morning job to a holiday job, to an intern, to an apprenticeship, to a manager, to the boardroom. An adult child of the King, growing in knowledge and authority, upright, a vibrant son or daughter enjoying our freedom, living and working from a place of rest.

No longer slaves

Research regarding slavery on the American plantations during the nineteenth century revealed that, even following Lincoln's great fight for its abolition, some slaves stayed on the plantations, expressing such feelings as, "At least here I am fed and have a roof over my head," or "I may be a slave, but I have some level of safety and security." Reflecting on this afterwards, I thought how this could have broken Lincoln's heart. His life's work had been to bring freedom to the slaves, yet they did not all take it. So like our reaction to God can be. Freedom is on offer, but we often shrink back. Following World War II, at the liberation of the concentration camps, there is footage of some of the prisoners coming out, seeing the bright lights of the cameras and the welcoming people coming to release them, then turning away and going back into the camp.

The offer of freedom can be very scary. Some offenders released from prison in the UK purposely go on to commit another crime in order to return, because prison is more familiar and less scary than freedom. When I was thinking about this, there was an animal programme on the television about what is called 'phased release'. Animals that had been kept either in captivity or in a sanctuary could not automatically be released into the wild as they lacked the skills to survive. God understands our needs and therefore He does not come along, release us and 'abandon' us to our freedom. One of the distorted pictures I realised I held in my heart was of a wide, open space where I was lost and abandoned. Who wants that?!

A fear of responsibility, or the lack of practice in making decisions, can also keep us as slaves. Abused or profoundly neglected babies, when adopted, are resistant to love because of deep fear and trauma. When we are adopted, we do not easily forget old ways. Older children, when adopted, often struggle with new ways of belonging. I was thinking about this when speaking to a friend of mine who had just taken a Great Dane from a rescue centre. The dog had been abused, and the friend said that it was nervous and seemed unable to trust them. He would keep away from them and growl at them when they went into the kitchen to feed him – yet cried all night when they went to bed, for fear of being abandoned. How like us. We cannot trust God and can be fearful of getting too close, yet frightened that He will leave us.

God does not want us like this; fearful, cringing slaves. The devil does. The devil may lose us to adoption, but he continues to try and make sure we do not live in the full inheritance of the 'royal' family. He will try and keep us fearful and not fully trusting our new Master.

Once, God gave our team a picture of some slaves and of church bells stuffed with cotton wool – depicting the enemy trying to ensure that we do not hear the bells, the bells of good news, the bells that welcome us to a new community, to church. Satan loves to keep us out of church, to isolate us. Or, if he cannot do that, he tries to get us to believe lies that we don't really belong, that we are outsiders or slaves. Slaves did not hear encouraging, loving words from their masters, they just heard "Do this" or "Don't do that". Do we think of God like this, just giving us instructions, making sure we behave ourselves and are keeping the Law? God wants intimate relationship, like the disciple John, leaning upon Jesus' chest, listening to His heartbeat.

You are not a mistake! God of all history intended you to be here – in this moment, this place – and wants to show love to you, speak to you and have a relationship with you. He is a good Father, and He speaks to us in language we can understand. God loves us and there is no intention of evil towards us. The code language of God is deciphered through the lens of God's continuing never-failing love for us. He communicates that to us throughout each day. When things go wrong, or when we do not understand, we need to automatically assume love and start from there. As a healed adopted child, we know who He is and know who we are, as with a Father and His children. We have an inheritance, with the promise that Jesus is with us through both the good and bad times.

In Ephesians Chapter one, Paul begins with our destiny from God: *"He chose us in him: to be holy and blameless."* Shame is not to be our experience, but freedom. Because of love, we are chosen to be adopted as His children through Jesus Christ. We are the focus of His love. We are meant to live our lives like heirs – children of a royal family – with security and confidence that 'all is well'. When, as rebellious, estranged and adopted children, we come 'home' again, or find our home for the first time – which is the royal palace – we come into a place of rest, security and peace. Forgiveness is the air we breathe; love is the pulsating heart at the centre of the household.

We will never be able to truly rest in our adoption and identity if we believe the lie that God is opposed to our humanity, our personhood. If we believe this, His power becomes a threat to us. We are frightened that, instead of restoring us to our true identity, He will take us over in such a way that we will have no permission to have any desires or thoughts of our own (in extreme cases we would almost cease to exist)! The truth is that God wants co-workers with whom He can share His plans and purposes. Co-workers means we move from our prisoner/slave mentality into knowing our identity as sons and daughters.

Another reason we can stay imprisoned is because we are waiting for a knight in shining armour to rescue us. There are no knights in shining armour. At some point I had realised that my husband, Ron, wasn't one and in fact could not be – nor should be. Very sad (!) though good news for him, but I was shocked when one day I felt Jesus saying, "I am not your knight in shining armour." What did that mean? I slowly realised that life was not a fairy story. Unlike Rapunzel, I could not throw my fantasised blonde hair out of the ivory tower that imprisoned me and have my knight climb up my hair to rescue me! That would have kept me powerless, passive, a victim, a damsel in distress. Meditating on this some years later, I revisited my fantasy. Jesus was in the tower with me, telling me to turn around and find the door (I was still wistfully looking out of the slit to the horizon waiting for my prince). The door appeared closed, but, when I pushed, it opened easily. I could see a deep, dark well ahead. Jesus said, "Step out." I gingerly did. Then a spiral staircase was revealed and Jesus said, "I am with you."

In John 15:15 Jesus says, *"I no longer call you servants, because a servant does not know his master's business. Instead, I have called you friends, for everything I have learned from my Father I have made known to you."* We are to serve God. The apostle Paul talked about himself as a servant of God; but this is not our primary identity: We are friends and sons or daughters of God who serve Him happily.

Galatians 5:25: *"Since we live by the Spirit, let us keep in step with the Spirit."* This is a very instructional verse. A servant or slave would hear, "Keep up, walk faster" and these instructions would lead to service. However, to a son or daughter it is about relationship – "Keep in step with me", "Come and walk with me, talk with me, join in, participate in my plans." When my eldest son was landscaping his garden, we would visit him and he and my husband would keep in step with one another; walk around, look at the garden and discuss the plans together.

Orphaned hearts

I want to now look at some of the thought patterns, behaviours and fears of those who, despite having been adopted by God, still have a slave like mentality, also described as an 'orphaned heart'.[44]

The orphan or servant has difficulty hearing the Father's voice because their main expectation will be to hear words of instruction or orders. Words of love and intimacy will not be expected. Usually when someone comes to tell me they cannot hear God, I ask them in what area are they are seeking guidance, because I know they have missed the truth that most of our conversations with God are intimate love talk. Slaves presumably only had conversations with their master when they were given further instructions.

Despite Jesus saying He would not leave us as orphans (John 14:18), when we still live with our orphan/slave/servant mentality, we remain insecure, suspicious of others, fearing they will get the scraps of attention and affirmation we desperately need. We are uncertain of provision and do not feel secure. We strive to become self-sufficient, often detached from our brothers and sisters in Christ because we see them as competitors. Whether we've been slaves in that we've got a victim mentality, or whether we have an orphan heart because of the lack of nurturing, we will not know how to live in the full inheritance of our adoption until we are healed.

When we are orphaned, we are lost yet remain self-reliant. We do not know how to ask. We rely on our own gifting and our own ability to look after ourselves. We are convinced that no-one else is trustworthy and that anything we want we must get for ourselves. We don't trust others, suspicious they will take advantage of us, be a block to our promotion, take our insights and information and use it for their self-gain.

When we trust someone and things go wrong or may not be done as we would like, then we find ourselves tempted to withdraw into our self-provision and self-reliance, resulting in solitary confinement, but we are made for connection.

Orphans live by the law. Like the Pharisees of Jesus' day, orphans try to relate to God on the basis of obeying the law, principles and regulations. When we have never had a healthy, loving relationship with either of our parents, at least the law is something to hold on to, whereas a relationship with an invisible person appears impossible. We would rather have a map than a guide. We look for the 'just tell me how to behave and what I must do' script. When I first became a Christian, I wanted someone to tell me what to do.

When we are orphaned, although we are insecure, we often become quite sinful in covering our insecurities by striving to act in the right way and do enough to please our brothers and sisters in Christ and hopefully earn God's blessings at the same time. Of course, we rarely experience an inward peace and rest because our inner world is filled with uncertainty, with the toxic cocktail of fearing trust and intimacy, whilst being terrified of abandonment.

We can become addicted to and continually strive for praise, approval and acceptance. This can also include striving for reassurance – 'Tell me who I am'. Never satisfied with the answer, this leads to further fear, failure, shame of our neediness and the risk of rejection. So we continue to cover our orphaned heart, and experience feelings of God being distant. We hide (cover our hearts) for fear of being seen and in order to protect ourselves.

As orphans, our motive for service is often the need for personal achievement. We are seeking to impress God and others and often may wish to be seen amongst the spiritually mature. This can cause quite an addiction to church involvement but when it doesn't work, we can lose our motivation and end up feeling quite apathetic. Our motivation for service, then, is ultimately self-serving.

When we are orphaned, despite our internal apathy, we may continue to appear vigilant in our disciplines, covering up our disappointment, weariness and lack of joy by trying to stimulate ourselves towards more prayer, more Bible reading, more study, etc. We can even find ourselves evaluating other people's spirituality by comparing ourselves in how much time we spend in prayer and reading the Bible. Yet as orphans we may be able to quote the Bible extensively whilst never experiencing the love and acceptance of Jesus.

Jesus spoke to the Pharisees about this problem saying, *"You search the scriptures because you think that in them you have eternal life. But the scriptures point to me, yet you refuse to come to me to receive this life."* John 5:39-40 (NLT) We cover up any mistakes, sins or faults we have made. We like to expose other people's difficulties in an attempt to hide our own. In an effort to make ourselves look good we try to make others look bad, giving anything positive said about that person a negative slant. Our relationships can be destructive with issues of control, criticism, possessiveness and lack of respect for others. As orphans we may have often suffered at the hands of authoritative figures and are therefore suspicious of any authority other than their own. Orphaned, we are mistrustful of anyone in authority, whether at home, work or church. We regard being subject to anyone else as being vulnerable to being used and abused again.

Our orphaned hearts are guarded, conditioned, and closed to receiving and giving unconditional love. We cover up any mistakes, fearful of the consequences of having done something wrong, and often lie to defend ourselves. We have a fear of exposure and punishment.

When we are orphans, we see God as a master who has to continually be kept happy, which I wrote about in Chapter 3. There is a direct correlation between how we see God and how we see ourselves.

We are eligible for all the Father has for us. As adopted children, we have an inheritance, but sometimes we are unable to live in the fulness of this truth. One cleaning lady I had was given a free holiday for her and her husband by one of the other couples she worked for. She only had to pay her fares and then could stay for free in a flat the couple owned in Spain. This Spanish resort had a large swimming pool with a very luxurious entrance. There was a notice which read something like 'private owners only' at the entrance, in the car park and at the entrance to the pool. This couple reasoned that as they weren't the owners, they shouldn't really be there, they weren't entitled to enjoy it, so would creep in and out to get a bus to the beach and they never entered the swimming pool area. We can live in the Kingdom like this.

I was at a conference a few years ago when the man on the platform spoke about his inability to enter into this full inheritance and how God had revealed this to him through a dream. In the dream the man had been called to a solicitor's office where he was told he was the sole beneficiary of a relative's will. He went to look at the property; a beautiful gatehouse, into which he gratefully moved. In the dream, some years later a cousin arrived and asked him why he was living in the gatehouse. The man became quite defensive and wanted to rush off and find the will when the cousin asked, "Why aren't you living in the great house?" In the dream the man saw he had only got as far as the gatehouse, which was merely the entrance to all he had inherited.

He then invited us to do a meditation on entering into the great house. I happily walked past the gatehouse into the big mansion, which was fine. But I only put the lights on in a couple of the rooms, because I was fearful I wouldn't be able to pay the electricity bill!

Charles Spurgeon (1834-1892) told this story from his personal experience. He was called to the home of an elderly woman who was bedridden and malnourished. During his visit, Spurgeon noticed a framed document on the wall. He asked the woman, "Is this yours?"
She said it was and explained that she had worked as a maid in the household of some of the English nobility. "Before Lady So-and-so died," the woman said, "she gave that to me. I served her for nearly half a century. I've been so proud of it because she gave it to me. I had it framed. It's been hanging on the wall ever since she died 10 years ago."
Mr Spurgeon asked, "Would you allow me to take it and have it examined more closely?"
"Oh yes," said the woman, who had never learned to read, "Just be sure I get it back."

Spurgeon took it to the authorities. They had been looking for it. It was a bequest. The English noblewoman had left her maid a home and money. This elderly woman lived in a little one-room house built out of wooden boxes and was starving to death – yet she had hanging on the wall a document that authorised her to be well cared for and to live in a fine house. The money was gathering interest. It belonged to her.

In conclusion, when we're orphaned, we relate to our peers through competition, rivalry and jealousy. We fear that if someone else advances, they will earn all the value and respect and we'll be overlooked again. Orphan hearts are indeed hearts held in bondage. We are a slave to fear and mistrust and we cover this with our independence and self-reliance, which of course, leads to loneliness. Orphans can have a false comfort in self-achievement until something goes wrong.

So, parts of us remain believing lies that keep us in that slave/orphaned mind set. We continually strive for praise and approval, rather than knowing we are totally accepted and can live in God's unconditional love.

We need to continually guard our hearts, otherwise we may behave more like the elder brother from Jesus' story of the prodigal son in Luke 15, not knowing everything the Father has is ours. And just imagine if you were trying to find the kingdom of love and met an elder brother, a slave, an orphaned minded person who gave you a list of instructions under the heading of obedience rather than introducing you to the King.

Living in God's love

Let's look now at what it is like to live in the truth of all God is offering us as an adopted child. Healthy children live by the law of love knowing that they can always rely on the Father's love. They understand that *"The one who learns to love has fulfilled every requirement."* Romans 13:8 (TPT). Sons and daughters expect words of affection and affirmation, plans for the future, conversation. Children not only expect to hear their father but also to be heard. I always finish speaking to my granddaughter Olivia with, "Love you" and she replies, "Love you too, Nanna."

There is an expectation to be involved in the family business (the Kingdom of God).

We need to always remember that of course things can go wrong, but we have to learn not to return to our former state of heart and mind. Healthy, adopted children of God see Him as a loving Father who accepts them unconditionally. They know that the love is not based upon their performance but is based on the One (God) whose nature is always to give and to love. Therefore a healthy child knows he doesn't have to earn Father's love, because He loves them completely just as they are. Also, He is never disappointed in us. He hasn't got the same unrealistic expectations of us that we have of ourselves.

Healthy children of God learn how to be interdependent. They know they need the community of love that God and the Body of Christ offers. This interdependence allows healthy children to give away that which they receive and allow love to flow through them. They understand their complete dependency on God, like Jesus when He says, *"The Son can do nothing of Himself, unless it is something He sees the Father doing, for whatever the Father does, these things the Son also does in like manner."* John 5:19 (NASB)

When we experience living in love, we begin to live in peace and rest. No longer influenced by internal turmoil or fear, there is no need to strive for approval. Nor need we grasp, or try to control others or situations. When we are able to receive God's love, we are motivated by a deep sense of gratitude which causes us to want to bless others and be obedient to a loving Father.

As adopted children of God, we are able to celebrate the pleasure and delight in being loved by the Father. But for this we need a deep revelation and a new motivation of love to replace the old motivation of duty, obligation and fear.

So, as children of God, we experience a love relationship. Knowing we are loved by God, we have a loving attitude to other brothers and sisters, and although we must not minimize faults or sins in one another, we are not tempted to maximise them to make ourselves feel better. We are not meant to cover up faults and sins, but we are meant to seek to restore individuals back into the fulness of the Body of Christ in a spirit of love and gentleness. When we know we are loved, we are able to be open about our own sins and faults and confess them knowing that we will be forgiven, cleansed and healed.

As healthy adopted children, we are able to love in an open, affectionate and transparent way. We are able to lay down our own agendas in order to build someone else up. When we know deep in our innermost being we've been adopted into the royal family of God, we can start to feel positive and affirmed because we know we are valuable and precious to our Father. When we make a mistake, feeling secure in the Father's love, we know that we can go to Him because no matter what's happened we're still in the family. We are 'God's mess'!

Imagine yourself having done something wrong as a child and being told off by a neighbour. Do you run home to Dad and tell him, knowing he will help you sort it out? If you came from a healthy family, this will have been your experience.

As adopted heirs to the kingdom we are able to feel secure in our own identity and position, we don't fear the success or advancement of others and we are able to sincerely rejoice in others' blessings and success. As children of God we experience freedom – freedom from fear, shame, humiliation and guilt, and no longer need to keep proving ourselves. And we understand our inheritance.

Compare this story to the lady who did not believe herself eligible for the swimming pool: Some friends of mine had been invited to collect some objects of value from the local Manor House for the church fete. A lady answered the door in an apron whom they assumed to be the cleaner. She took them to collect the items, and they got talking about the good cause the money from the sale of the goods was going to. She then started to give them more trinkets, candlesticks, etc. One of my friends wanted to blurt out, "Are you allowed to do this; do you have the authority?" But then they realised she was the lady of the Manor House. In a similar way, we need to think of ourselves as children of God with a servant heart.

In order to have a healthy vision and knowledge of our inheritance, it is vital that we understand our identity, who we are in Christ. Jesus at His baptism knew He was beloved before He began His ministry. Identity precedes destiny. Ministry that does not have this security is fired by spiritual ambition and often a drive towards power because, as orphans, we feel we have to fight for everything that we need, whereas as sons and daughters of the King of Kings, we know we have everything we need for the journey towards rest.

As we discover our true selves, our identity, we start to cooperate with God's original design and fulfil our destiny, which is one of living in the fullness of our adoption. So much of our identity and inheritance links back to our listening to God. Remember in the previous Chapter, in John 13:23, the disciple Jesus loved was reclining next to Jesus – he leaned back on Jesus' chest. John describes himself as the one whom Jesus loves. We likewise can say:

I am the chosen one.
I am a daughter/son of the King.
I am a priest in a royal priesthood.
I am loved.
I am His beloved.

We need to be defined by who God says we are. Romans 8:17 (TPT): *"And since we are his true children, we qualify to share all his treasures, for indeed we are heirs of God himself. And since we are joined to Christ, we also inherit all that he is and all that he has. We will experience being co-glorified with him provided we accept his suffering as our own."*

So we look to God, not people, for:
His reassurance
His affirmation of us
His comfort.

I was on Premier Radio at the end of July and wrote in my prayer journal that not many of my friends and support group were able to listen and Jesus immediately said, "I listened." I said, "Oh yes, I am sorry – so sorry. I forgot you would be listening. How did I do?" "How do you think you did?" He asked. And I replied, "I think I did well."

Being right with God does not mean we are totally perfect. It does not mean we have no weaknesses or flaws. Righteousness, or the right way of being what God wishes and desires, is not a result of what we do but what Jesus has done for us. 2 Corinthians 3:17-20, *"Now the Lord is the Spirit, and where the Spirit of the Lord is, there is freedom. And we, who with unveiled faces all reflect the Lord's glory, are being transformed into his likeness with ever-increasing glory, which comes from the Lord, who is the Spirit."*

Since God alone possesses the secret of my identity, He alone can make me who I am and continues to make me who I will be. Not to cooperate with this is to refuse the fullness of my existence. Unlike all other created things, God gives us the freedom to become ourselves or not. He gives the invitation to enjoy the abundant life of being a royal daughter/son.

At the end of Ephesians 1 in the Message it says, *"The church, you see, is not peripheral to the world, the world is peripheral to the church. The church is Christ's body, in which he speaks and acts, by which he fills everything with his presence."* Whilst meditating on this, I had a picture of a beautiful royal palace with a heart pulsating with love and breathing forgiveness.

We are told in Romans 8:15 that God adopts us into this royal family as His beloved sons and daughters. As I have written, in biblical times when an adolescent 'became of age', the father would take his daughter or son into the marketplace and declare, "This is my beloved child in whom I am well pleased." They were then ready to enter the family business. When we are adopted by God, our identity becomes 'beloved child' and the family business is the kingdom manifesto; to do the same work as Jesus. We are given a family business debit card on which is written the name Jesus, where all God's promises are a "Yes and Amen" in Jesus (2 Corinthians 1:20).

So we are adopted into Christ's body where our new nature starts to be revealed. We arrive in the kingdom, royal palace, centre of the world, with our lungs filled with polluted unbelief (Ephesians 2, MSG) and have resurrected life breathed into us. God begins to make us uniquely the person whom he always intended us to be.

Whilst continuing to meditate on these amazing truths – Christ's love, the centre of the world, a pulsating heart of love as the centre, a royal palace which I could see – I got very excited about the beautiful centre of the world being Christ's domain. I thought, "Why isn't everyone clamouring to enter?" In my mind's eye I had pictures of refugees queuing at embassies to get passports to a better, safer place, so why isn't everyone queuing for their adoption papers? God said, "The palace is invisible to your physical eyes." Both our identity and our destiny.

God's promise to us: "From now on you will not be defined by who others say you are, not defined by malicious gossip or your own negative self-talk. No longer will you be named by the wound of childhood. Learn to walk in your true identity – princes and princesses in a royal palace; patients in a royal hospital; aliens and outcasts who have found sanctuary; fearful ones who have found a safe asylum." (Taken from my prayer journal.)

PRAYER

Father,

I do recognise much of my heart is still disabled by orphan thoughts and behaviours. I know my first step towards healing is to stop trying to fix myself, and to come to you.

Please set me free from the lies I believe about you and my sisters and brothers.

I do want to fully enter into the royal palace so I pray you will show me my adoption papers.

Help me to walk in my true identity.

Amen

Chapter 5

SELF-ACCEPTANCE

Instead of using the imagery of being adopted in a royal family to become adult sons and daughters of the King of Kings, Martin Luther uses a different symbolic story. It's called "The Freedom of a Christian". It's the story of a wealthy king (representing Jesus) who marries a debt-ridden prostitute (representing us).

The girl could never make herself a queen. But then the king comes along full of love for her. And on their wedding day he makes his marriage vow to her. With that, she is his, and the prostitute becomes a queen. He takes her, takes responsibility for her debts and she now shares his boundless wealth and status.

It is not that she earned it. She didn't become queen by behaving royally. Indeed, she doesn't know how to behave royally. But when the king made his marriage promise, he changed her status. For all her street ways, the girl is now a queen. She has been affirmed with a new identity, new authority and a new destiny and an intimacy with the loving king who is her husband.

"By the wedding ring of faith, He shares in the sins, death, and pains of hell which are His bride's," Martin Luther wrote as his very first image to explain the good news of the gospel. *"As a matter of fact, (Christ) makes (our sins) His own,"* he wrote. *"Here this rich and divine bridegroom Christ marries this poor, wicked harlot, redeems her from all her evil, and adorns her with all His goodness. Her sins cannot now destroy her, since they are laid upon Christ and swallowed up by Him."*

"Who then can fully appreciate what this royal marriage means?" Luther begs the believer to take hold of the incomprehensible: *"Who can understand the riches of the glory of this grace?... And she has that righteousness in Christ, her husband – of which she may boast as her own and which she can confidently display alongside her sins in the face of death and hell and say, 'If I have sinned, yet my Christ, in whom I believe, has not sinned, and all His is mine and all mine is His.'"*[45]

When some friends of mine became engaged, the future wife confessed to some credit card debts. She had been a single mum for a long time. The future husband replied, "Your debt becomes my debt. I can pay it."

Martyn Lloyd Jones said, *"Ultimately it comes down to this, the real cause of our trouble is our failure to realise our union with Christ."* We become one – with Him. Christ within, the hope of glory. His inheritance – our inheritance.

But all these truths, our adoption by our Heavenly Father, our marriage union to Jesus, His indwelling presence, do not fully help us if we do not accept ourselves. Imagine if we as the newly married bride, or long married wife, or as the daughter or son of the King, don't really believe this and are unable to live in all that has been lavished on us. What if we continue to disapprove of ourselves, judge ourselves, still see ourselves as the harlot or orphan. Yes, it's been offered but are we able to receive it? Or do we accept it but then start in subtle ways to try and repay the gift?

It is not enough to know we are accepted in Christ. We have to learn to accept ourselves in Him. When we don't accept ourselves, believe ourselves not eligible, we believe lies like:

I shouldn't be here in the royal palace.
I don't belong with this group.
I am a fraud. (imposter syndrome)
I must continually ask what the rules are.
I must be careful not to be noticed.
I must be careful not to make a mistake.

We think it's best to hide – never go into the throne room myself but continually rely on others to tell me what to do. As I wrote in the previous Chapter, often we meet the elder brother who is very willing to tell us what to do.

In the project of becoming a whole human being in Christ, self-acceptance is critical. Why? First, because without self-acceptance we cannot truly practice God's presence. Aligning with God's acceptance of us has ushered us into a new place of hearing His voice: and once a disciple can hear the Father's voice, all manner of healing and becoming are possible. We listen as a son or daughter to the love talk, not as an orphan for instructions. Imagine if our Martin Luther queen, every time the king called for her, thought it was to command her to do something rather than saying, "Come sit with me, let me enjoy your company".

Self-acceptance is not self-promotion, neither is it an idealising of self 'because I'm worth it', nor is it self-realisation and selfish individualism.

Misunderstanding self-acceptance makes us think that it will lead to self-absorption/self-obsession; that we'll find ourselves continually analysing, measuring, comparing ourselves to others or our illusory 'ought-to-be' person. In fact, the reverse is true. Romans 8:6 (MSG): *"Obsession with self in these matters is a dead end, attention to God leads us out into the open, into a spacious free life."*

The more we accept ourselves, the less we think about ourselves. We find out who we are and what we are living for.

Ephesians 1:11-12 (MSG): *"It's in Christ that we find out who we are and what we are living for. Long before we first heard of Christ and got our hopes up, he had his eye on us, had designs on us for glorious living, part of the overall purpose he is working out in everything and everyone."*

The other stumbling block is the thinking that self-acceptance gives us an excuse to keep on sinning. Dr Pamela Evans writes, "Some Christians find the whole concept of self-esteem (also called self-worth, self-regard) rather disturbing. In fact, some speak as if having a self is, in itself, sinful. Psychologically speaking, my 'self' is my sense of my own existence. To recognize I have a self does not mean that I am automatically selfish. I do need to watch my attitude to self, but it is not God's plan that I try to annihilate it in order to have no self at all, as some seem to believe. The Biblical picture is that we are to put off the 'old self' and put on the 'new self', created to be like God in righteousness and holiness (Ephesians 4:22-24)."[46]

The Message puts Ephesians 4:20-24 this way, *"You learned Christ! My assumption is that you have paid careful attention to him, been well instructed in the truth precisely as we have it in Jesus. Since, then, we do not have the excuse of ignorance, everything – and I do mean everything – connected with that old way of life has to go. It's rotten through and through. Get rid of it! And then take on an entirely new way of life – a God-fashioned life, a life renewed from the inside and working itself into your conduct as God accurately reproduces his character in you."*

What this adds up to then is no more lies, no more pretence. In essence, to die to the old and live to the new. What we accept is our true self, what the Bible calls our new nature – the Christ within – that part of us that is made for eternity and is going to live forever, which is both human and divine. When we are broken or imprisoned by lies, we switch this truth believing the lie that everything bad, horrible and defective is the real me, and what we are really like, and the 'good' in us is pretence and fraudulent.

I heard a good example of this one year at a Christian festival. The speaker was telling the story of why he was having to speak without notes. He'd been having trouble with his bank, and whilst on the phone he was waving his arms about in exasperation. This resulted in him knocking over and spilling his coffee all over his laptop which then stopped working. He swore. He told this story from the stage but then said, "It is amazing how the real you pops up under pressure."

I thought, "That is not the real you, that is old nature/false self. The real you is your new nature."

As Dr Pamela Evans writes, "God's plan is not to annihilate our self. But there are many prayers and statements that would lead us to believe the opposite."[47]

There is a story told by Terry Virgo, who is a great communicator. He was asked to preach at a small village Baptist church. Because of his popularity they had to wait 18 months for him to be available. Before the event they advertised the morning service in the other local villages and had a morning congregation three times bigger than its normal size.

When Terry Virgo arrived, he went with the elders into the vestry to pray. The first prayer was along the lines, "We thank you Father for Terry but we just want to hear you, Jesus." The second person prayed, "Yes, we want nothing of Terry – just you." At this, Terry Virgo stopped the prayer meeting and asked them, "Would you like me to stay in the vestry and just yell through the keyhole?"

When I was first a Christian, this way of thinking deeply confused me and led me to think I had to 'kill off' myself completely. In church once I was in front of a woman with a beautiful singing voice. At the end of the service I turned and complimented her on her voice, saying how lovely she sounded. To which she put one hand on her heart, the other up to heaven and said, "Oh, it wasn't me", unable to accept the gift God had given her.

When John the Baptist said, "I must decrease," he was referring to his ministry, not his personhood.

Mark Twain wrote, *"A man cannot be comfortable without his own approval."* It is God who made us. He alone knows our true identity. He affirms us, shows us bits about ourselves. He says, "Lin, I made you to be able to do, create, think this as well as that. Do not limit My making of you." We are His masterpieces. We must begin with God – we only exist because God wills we exist. He made/created us and loves us. When we don't accept ourselves, we try to impress with all our best efforts of keeping the law.

Galatians 2:19-21 (MSG): *"…I tried keeping rules and working my head off to please God, and it didn't work. So I quit being a 'law man' so that I could be God's man. Christ's life showed me how, and enabled me to do it. I identified myself completely with Him. Indeed, I have been crucified with*

Christ. My ego is no longer central. It's not important that I appear righteous before you or have your good opinion, and I am no longer driven to impress God. Christ lives in me. The life you see me living is not 'mine,' but it is lived by faith in the Son of God, who loved me and gave himself for me. I am not going back on that.

"Is it not clear to you that to go back to that old rule-keeping, peer-pleasing religion would be an abandonment of everything personal and free in my relationship with God? I refuse to do that, to repudiate God's grace. If a living relationship with God could come by rule-keeping, then Christ died unnecessarily."

Oswald Chambers, when speaking on verse 20, says, *"What Christ did for us on the cross is then done in us. The life we now live (not the life we long to live, or pray to live) but the life we now live by the faith of the Son of God."*

This faith is not Paul's faith in Jesus but the faith Jesus has put in him, and this is the self we accept. Our true self is our new nature. Old nature is false, pretence, 'image' stuff. Jesus comes, lives in our real essential person. That hidden part of us that possibly, to begin with, only we know about and can be frightened of and fearful to show others – that is our true self. This is the self we accept, so not 'non-existence', nor 'this is me, warts and all'.

To explain this in pictorial language, the person God created us to be is a butterfly. Caterpillars cannot imagine it is possible to fly, and when we are stuck in our old nature, we believe that a caterpillar is who we really are. Learning to believe we are a butterfly, while all around us other caterpillars want us to remain with them, is a great challenge. We once had a cartoon on the kitchen wall with two caterpillars looking up at a butterfly, saying to each other, "You wouldn't get me up in one of those flying machines."

To become all God intends us to be, we need to fly. The lack of self-acceptance keeps us hiding, under the law and not fulfilling our potential.

2 Corinthians 3:7-18 (MSG): *"The Government of Death, its constitution chiselled on stone tablets, had a dazzling inaugural. Moses' face as he delivered the tablets was so bright that day (even though it would fade soon enough) that the people of Israel could no more look right at him than stare into the sun. How much more dazzling, then, the Government of Living Spirit?*

"If the Government of Condemnation was impressive, how about the Government of Affirmation? Bright as that old government was, it would look downright dull alongside this new one. If that makeshift arrangement impressed us, how much more this brightly shining government installed for eternity?

"With that kind of hope to excite us, nothing holds us back. Unlike Moses, we have nothing to hide. Everything is out in the open with us. He wore a veil so the children of Israel wouldn't notice that the glory was fading away – and they didn't notice. They didn't notice it then and they don't notice it now, don't notice that there's nothing left behind that veil. Even today when the proclamations of that old, bankrupt government are read out, they can't see through it. Only Christ can get rid of the veil so they can see for themselves that there's nothing there.

"Whenever, though, they turn to face God as Moses did, God removes the veil and there they are – face to face! They suddenly recognize that God is a living, personal presence, not a piece of chiselled stone. And when God is personally present, a living Spirit, that old, constricting legislation is recognized as obsolete. We're free of it! All of us! Nothing between us and God, our faces shining with the brightness of his face. And so we are transfigured much like the Messiah, our lives gradually becoming brighter and more beautiful as God enters our lives and we become like him."

2 Corinthians 3:15-18 in the NRSV says, *"Indeed, to this very day whenever Moses is read, a veil lies over their minds; but when one turns to the Lord, the veil is removed. Now the Lord is the Spirit, and where the Spirit of the Lord is, there is freedom. And all of us, with unveiled faces, seeing the glory of the Lord as though reflected in a mirror, are being transformed into the same image from one degree of glory to another; for this comes from the Lord, the Spirit."*

C S Lewis writes, *"We are always completely, and therefore equally, known to God... We have unveiled. Not that any veil could have baffled His sight. The change is in us. The passive changes to the active. Instead of merely being known, we show, we tell, we offer ourselves to view."*[48]

So this false self – old nature – wraps itself around our true self – the bit we need to learn to accept. The false self is a classic codependent. We are often out of touch with our feelings, needs and desires. The false self suppresses or camouflages feelings, making emotional honesty impossible. Needing to present a perfect image so that everyone will admire us. No one else knows us. We wear as many faces as we have friends.

The false self has a highly skilled defensive radar in order to avoid feelings of rejection by never risking true intimacy. It is a fear-based centre. When we suffer from shame, we are imprisoned by the lie we are defective and so keep our false self alive. Instead of revealing, we cover, in order to make up for this often imagined defectiveness. We build up a dishonest self-image or at least make no attempt to honestly self-reveal. We are unable to show and tell.

We do not want other people to see us because they will learn our shameful secret or our shameful past. Memories are often wrapped in the feelings of shame – this does not mean it was our fault. Memories are confused between what has been done to us and what we have done. Either way, we experience shameful feelings around this incident. Just because we sometimes behave badly does not make us bad. To risk becoming our true selves is life-changing. John Eagen writes, *"Define yourself radically as one beloved by God."*

In order to accept ourselves, we need to understand that God, as our creator, created good things. As I have written in Chapter four, the person God created me to be and become, God's original blueprint, is deeper and precedes my sin nature.

As beloved by God, we are to display our new nature created in God's likeness – righteous, holy and true. However who we believe we are, affects what we do. If we believe we are 'an old rotten sinner' then we will just keep sinning or feel permanently joyless and guilty. We are frightened to be our true self with God. We censor our prayers then wonder why we lack intimacy.

Thomas Merton writes, *"To say I was born in sin is to say I came into the world with a false self. I came into existence under a sign of contradiction, being someone I was never meant to be and therefore a denial of what I am supposed to be."*[49]

Therefore, seeing ourselves as nothing but a sinner results in us giving sin more power. If we focus on the truth we have been put right with Christ – 'we are the righteousness of Christ' – we will focus on Jesus and all He is doing in and through us. When we believe we are right with God, the automatic response is to do right. To quote Joyce Meyer, *"We need a 'righteousness consciousness' not a 'sin consciousness.'"*

For me to be a saint means to be myself. The journey towards wholeness is finding out who I am and discovering my true self. Focus on feeding and growing that part of you. Thoughts like, "If they really knew me", or "Why am I afraid to tell them who I really am?" reveal we are living a lie. It is a distorted idea to believe when God looks at us, He just sees Jesus. This conveys the idea that Jesus is covering us because God cannot look upon such rotten sinners. The freedom from the slavery of sin is much like our freedom from legalism. We need to allow the Holy Spirit to reveal who we really are and are going to become. We focus on Him.

We go to the person who knows us. We are known by God. So we must learn to overcome – deliberately choose to forsake – our old, unaccepting and unloving attitudes toward the self and to bring every thought subject to Christ (2 Corinthians 10:5). We then begin to see ourselves, not through our eyes, or even through the eyes of others, but through God's loving, accepting eyes. We therefore begin to learn and to exercise the virtue of patience and gentleness towards ourselves, as well as towards others.

Some of us so fear facing the truth about ourselves because we believe the lie that we are more sinful or viler than others – or somehow not normal – so we hide, fearful of both solitude, because of our inner loneliness, and also fearful of intimacy and companionship with others, because of shame.[50] But to come to a place of self-acceptance we must go to God, who is truly love.

Romans 8:15-16 (TPT): *"And you did not receive the 'spirit of religious duty,' leading you back into the fear of never being good enough. But you have received the 'Spirit of Full Acceptance,' enfolding you into the family of God. And you will never feel orphaned, for as he rises up within us, our spirits join him in saying the words of tender affection, 'Beloved Father, Abba!' For the Holy Spirit makes God's fatherhood real to us as he whispers into our innermost being: 'You are God's beloved child!' And since we are his true children, we qualify to share all his treasures! Indeed, we are heirs of God Himself, and since we are joined to the Anointed One, we inherit all that he is and all that he has."*

C S Lewis wrote, *"The question is not what we intended ourselves to be, but what He intended us to be when He made us. He is the inventor; we are only the machine. He is the painter; we are only the picture. We may be content to remain what we call 'ordinary people', but He is determined to carry out a quite different plan. To shrink back from that plan is not humility; it is laziness and cowardice. To submit to it is not conceit or megalomania; it is obedience."*[51]

On reading this God spoke to me, saying, "Let me go deeper into releasing you. I need you to shine more – I need more of you. Let me shape your uniqueness. Relax – Let Me."

Humility

Before we move on to look at some of the symptoms of a lack of self-acceptance, we need to explore the virtue of humility as opposed to false humility, which includes self-deprecation and false modesty.

Humility allows us to see our weaknesses, shortcomings and sin without losing hope. As I have written, our true selves do not live in sinless perfection, nor are we perfect in the way we would like to be. All of our failures, errors and mistakes are part of who we are at the moment, and they need not depress us. Because humility keeps us rooted in and focused on the grace of God, I have written more on this subject in "Father Matters".

Humility is not an inferiority complex. We simply accept our God's view of us and this humility leads to a deep peace and rest in our innermost being. We are at home within ourselves.

A few months ago, I was on a course where I felt overlooked, misunderstood and not heard. Internally, I blamed and complained about the leader and the course. I then berated myself for not being able to cope. I tried speaking out and felt disruptive. I stayed silent and felt unauthentic. I tried to persevere but, in the end, I left the course when I accepted for me it was too damaging. I acknowledged to God my weaknesses. I 'gave up' and was flooded with peace.

Dr Pamela Evans in "Shaping the Heart" writes, "*Humility allows God to be God and enthrones Jesus as King.*" Dallas Williard describes humility as, "*Trusting God and not trying to control the outcome.*" Humility means we no longer labour under the heavy yoke of who we should be or what we should do. If we know, as far as we are able, that our heart and motives are pure and transparent before God, then we don't have to worry about our reputation. If we face the truth about ourselves – that we are a 'work in progress' – then we can self-reveal – "Yes, I messed up then", "Yes, I didn't tell the whole truth", "Yes, I did have an extra drink". Then the more we do this, the less the enemy can come with accusations and condemnation. We can't impress God, and we need to learn to stop trying to impress others – and ourselves! When we don't accept ourselves, we struggle not to be controlled by what others think, or how we think we should be. The more we struggle with this, the more likely we are to follow rules and laws – keeping safe, appearing good – rather than to follow Jesus, a grace-filled relationship.

I am the righteousness of God in Jesus Christ

Romans 3:21-26 (MSG): *"But in our time something new has been added. What Moses and the prophets witnessed to all those years has happened. The God-setting-things-right that we read about has become Jesus-setting-things-right for us. And not only for us, but for everyone who believes in him. For there is no difference between us and them in this. Since we've compiled this long and sorry record as sinners (both us and them) and proved that we are utterly incapable of living the glorious lives God wills for us, God did it for us. Out of sheer generosity he put us in right standing with himself.*

"A pure gift. He got us out of the mess we're in and restored us to where he always wanted us to be. And he did it by means of Jesus Christ. God sacrificed Jesus on the altar of the world to clear that world of sin. Having faith in him sets us in the clear. God decided on this course of action in full view of the public – to set the world in the clear with himself through

the sacrifice of Jesus, finally taking care of the sins he had so patiently endured. This is not only clear, but it's now – this is current history! God sets things right. He also makes it possible for us to live in his rightness."

"I am the righteousness of God in Jesus Christ." The more we live in this truth the more we are set free from the burden of not being acceptable. When we understand this, we no longer live in guilt and condemnation.

Leanne Payne writes, *"The true self is the self that abides in Christ and collaborates with Him, the justified new creation, the soul that is saved and lives eternally, which we joyfully and in great humility and thankfulness accept."*

Leanne goes on to write, *"The acceptance of oneself, like all that is valued in the Christian faith can never be a second-hand experience. We must, each of us, apprehend Christ and the fulness of His salvation for ourselves. To so apprehend Him is to come into our full uniqueness."*

"Self-acceptance is critical because we cannot offer a love to others that we have not appropriated ourselves. As we practice His presence, we discover a more tender, compassionate and wise love in our heart toward all those God calls us to minister to." It is a virtue of self-acceptance that enables us to *"celebrate our inadequacy, our smallness, knowing Christ to be our full sufficiency"* as well as to pass affirmation on to others, to *"see and call forth the real person to others."*

"For any of us the first intentional step into self-acceptance comes through knowing ourselves as fallen and in need of forgiveness through Christ. "The humility that acknowledges ourself as truly fallen is a first priority in coming to accept

ourself... The humble acceptance of myself as fallen but now justified by Another, who is my righteousness, is the basis on which I can accept myself, learn to laugh at myself, be patient with myself. And then, wonder of wonders, be enabled for at least part of the time to forget myself."[52]

Acceptance of the self is best understood as a virtue because it will not be automatically acquired in the process of living but must be pursued and cultivated. Then, as we spend time in God's presence, our heart and mind become aligned with His. We begin to see God, ourselves, and the people and situations we're concerned about from God's perspective. Our hearts 'tune in' to His as we pray, causing us to feel His compassion, sense his pleasure, or mourn with Him for our world.

We choose not to see ourselves or others through our negative view but ask God how He sees us. My husband and I were at the Hilton some years ago. We had been invited to a lunch with the Duke of Edinburgh. My husband was a paper merchant, and his company had donated some paper to a charity where the Duke of Edinburgh was the patron, so we were invited to this lunch as special guests. Because we were special guests, we were going to meet the Duke at a drinks reception before the luncheon. I was standing there whilst others were waiting for Prince Philip to arrive and I was thinking to myself, "This is amazing – they don't know that I'm a princess; they don't know that I am a daughter of the King of Kings."

We all need to know this. You need to know that we are royal, that we are royalty. It may be invisible to this world, but nevertheless it is true – we are royal. We are princes and princesses. We need to know, deep down Who we belong to – our Heavenly Father, the King of Kings and therefore we are part of a royal family. Our crowns fall off when we look down in introspection, self-analysis and self-consciousness.

Brian Draper gives us a wonderful example of self-acceptance in the story of Angelina Jolie:

"Let's face it: on the surface of things, Angelina Jolie is beautiful. That's how most of us have known and judged her, anyway: Angelina, the beautiful actress.
Of course, she's so much more than that. In fact, her acting roles in recent times have traded less heavily on her looks, and she's worked passionately as a UN goodwill ambassador for many years. But still: it was a deeply brave thing, personally and professionally, for her to announce the news back in 2013 of her preventative double mastectomy.
'I choose not to keep my story private,' she wrote in her New York Times op-ed article, 'because there are many women who do not know that they might be living under the shadow of cancer. It is my hope that they, too, will be able to get gene tested, and that they will know that they have strong options.' In so doing, she becomes an icon of something rather different from the usual shimmering superficial superstardom.
The Japanese have an ancient craft known as *kintsugi*. If a piece of valuable china such as a vase or bowl was dropped, then instead of throwing it away, or repairing it perfectly, the *kintsugi* craftspeople would use lacquer containing gold to piece it back together. And so, while the original work was made whole again, its scars and cracks were kept, celebrated, honoured, in golden seams. And the restored item was considered far more beautiful than the original — because of its brokenness.
Perhaps, in not hiding the scars of her recent breakage and reconstruction, Jolie's beauty is similarly transformed: an on-screen vision of perfection yielding to a truer, breaking

beauty that we all, in fact, possess, if we did but dare to see it in ourselves and those around us."

The Japanese word *wabi* means simplicity and *sabi* means the 'beauty of age and wear'. It is a view centred on the acceptance of change and imperfection. In Japan, there is a respect for these views.

To begin to walk in self-acceptance

To approach this from a different angle, we can say one of the main symptoms of a lack of self-acceptance is the fear of not being good enough – not having what it takes. We fear we are not acceptable to God, people or ourselves.

Pride and shame both masquerade as humility. They are bullies which make demands as 'shoulds' and 'oughts'. I should have been better, done better. I don't measure up. I lack. When we don't approve/accept ourselves, we project this on to God and think He doesn't approve of us.

St Augustine wrote, *"How can I grow close to God if I am far from myself?"* To begin to walk in self-acceptance, I must have peace with God. I must believe that He loves me. He does not wait until I am perfected to love me; He loves me unconditionally and completely at all times. Secondly, I must RECEIVE His love. He is never going to love me more than he does right now. The difference is that as I grow and change, I will know that love.

Receiving is a big issue. When we receive from God we actually take into ourselves what He is offering. As we receive His love we then have love in us. Once we are filled with God's love we can begin loving ourselves. Then, and only then, can we also begin giving that love back to God and bestowing it on other people. We cannot give away what we don't have! *"We can't love others if there is no self to do the loving."* (Roberta Bondi)

Romans 5:5 says that God's love has been poured out in our hearts through the Holy Spirit who has been given to us. That simply means that when the Lord – in the form of the Holy Spirit – comes to dwell in our heart because of our faith in His Son, Jesus Christ, He brings love with Him, because God is love (1 John 4:8).

We all need to ask ourselves what we are doing with the love of God that has been freely given to us. Are we rejecting it because we don't think we are valuable enough to be loved? Feeling worthless? (which is shame and is not the antidote to pride) Expecting to be thrown away, useless?

Do we believe God is like other people who have rejected and hurt us? Or are we receiving His love by faith, believing that He is greater than our failures and weaknesses? What kind of relationship do you have with God, with yourself and with your fellow man? Ultimately if we believe we are useless and worthless we think others must believe the same – or they are just using us – or being charitable.

It never occurred to me that I even had a relationship with myself. It was just something I never thought of until God began teaching me in these areas. I now realise that I spend more time with myself than with anyone else (!) and it is vital that I get along with me! You are the one person you never get away from!

We all know how agonising it is to work day after day with someone we don't get along with, but at least we don't have to take that person home with us at night. But we are with us all the time, day and night. We never have one minute away from ourselves, not even one second – therefore, it is of the utmost importance that we have peace with ourselves!"[53]

We often know we have a problem with love, but we do not know that our problem has roots. We frequently try to deal with the bad fruit in our lives (symptoms) – we must try harder, love more, etc – and never get to the root cause of it. If the root remains the fruit will keep coming back. No matter how many times we cut it off, eventually it will come back. This cycle is frustrating. We are trying the best we know how, and yet it seems we never find a permanent solution to our miseries.

Do you like yourself? Love yourself? Accept yourself? Most people don't like themselves, you know. I have many years' experience with people, trying to help them to be whole emotionally, mentally, spiritually and socially, and have simply discovered that most people really don't like themselves! Some of them know it, while others don't even have a clue that it's the root of many problems in their life. It's one of the 'stations' of healing and I cover the different aspects of it in my books: "Father Matters" on father wounds, "Mother Matters" on mother wounds, "Sorry Matters" on forgiveness and confession.

It is not enough to know that God accepts us if we don't accept ourselves. Shame, self-rejection and even self-hatred, are the root causes of many relationship problems. God wants us to have great relationships. I have found the Bible to be a book about relationships; I find teaching in it about my relationship with God, with other people and with myself. Triune God is relational, and we are made for relationship.

1 Peter 3:11 tells us to not merely desire peaceful relations with God, with our fellowmen, and with ourself, but to pursue, go after them. God's word instructs us to have good relationships, but it also teaches us how to develop and maintain those relationships.

Romans 5:1-2: *"Therefore, since we have been justified through faith, we have peace with God through our Lord Jesus Christ, through whom we have gained access by faith into this grace in which we now stand. And we boast in the hope of the glory of God."*

Stop worrying about whether God is pleased with you! Stop striving to try and please Him.

Self-acceptance in relationships

Learning to live in peace and self-acceptance affects our relationship with others. If as a mother we are unable to accept ourselves as loveable as a woman and embrace our femininity, we will have a strained relationship with any daughters we may have. If we are locked in shame and self-hatred, we will not accept the love offered by any friends or partners. We will judge their motives: they are just being kind to me because they are Christians; I am a charity project. Or with a partner, there must be something wrong with them also to be with me.

Consider a couple who came to see me. Both Christians, they had married after six months of knowing each other. He loved art, theatre, art galleries and was setting up a website to encourage Christian art, etc. He was self-absorbed and egotistical. She said how much she loved art, visited everywhere with him, and on marriage, became a cofounder of a charity they set up to promote 'the arts' in churches.

She came from a family unable to express views or emotions – very suppressed with outbursts of anger. He came from a family with an angry, controlling father. Within months, it transpired the wife had stopped going to art galleries, etc. She was bored and wasn't interested in it all, but didn't know what she did like. She had completely bent in, become a chameleon in order to try and find love. He liked the fact that he could originally control her by teaching her all he knew but now he found he was controlling someone with very little substance. Neither had experienced anything like authentic love. The opposite of love isn't hatred, it is cold indifference or being used. Using someone to get our love needs met.

We all long to be loved for who we are, who we really are, and not for whatever it is that may please someone else. Because of the husband's childhood, he had been badly treated by his father. All he could offer was his expertise, which he used to bolster his 'hidden' view of himself. When that was rejected by his wife, he became angry and even more controlling. She became frightened and less and less able to work out what she really wanted. Easier to appease him and remain a non-person – which of course didn't satisfy him. At the core, they both considered themselves unlovable. When we have been mistreated, it isn't just the wounds that damage us but the lies the wounds cause us to believe about ourselves.

Jesus came to bind up the broken hearted and set the captives free and these two promises of Jesus are often linked. One of the reasons our hearts are slow to heal is because we believe lies about ourselves. Lies inflamed by the enemy. 'The father of lies' imprisons us. It isn't just our broken hearts which are in need of help, it is that the break/wound often causes us to have a distorted view of ourselves and God. We judge and blame ourselves or start to have a wrong view of God. We fail to exercise compassion towards ourselves.

God tells us to love our neighbour as ourselves. When we don't like ourselves, don't accept ourselves, judge ourselves and believe the lie that God sees us as we see ourselves, we are not able to love our neighbour from an authentic place.

A friend of mine, now in her late forties, whilst at university was dating the worship leader in the local church. They visited each other's respective parents, prayed with others and spoke about their future together. They encouraged each other that they would not only marry but have a ministry together. One day he told her that God had said she was not right for him.

I personally don't think God said that. I think he was unable to be straightforward and say he had changed his mind. What happened was, not only was she deeply wounded, heartbroken, still describing him as her love, but she believed the lie that God thought she was not good enough for him – that there was something wrong with her. She felt God saw her as defective in some way and that is how she saw herself. She had a very harsh view of herself and God. She lacked compassion towards herself and did not know a compassionate God.

Ephesians 6:14: *"Stand firm then, with the belt of truth buckled around your waist, with the breastplate of righteousness in place."*

This is not magic armour. It does no good if this breastplate of God's approval is covering up the internal lies of self-rejection, self-hatred and negative self-talk. We need to get to the place where we can say, "I like myself. I don't always like everything I do or say – but I am a work in progress. Jesus hasn't finished with me yet."

So let's take our next steps on the journey of self-acceptance that will ultimately lead to the journey of rest. If you are ready to take the journey, open your heart to God's grace, let Him reveal truth to you and ask for a gift of patience.

STEP 1 – Stop worrying about what others think

When we fear we are not 'good enough', we don't have what it takes, then we fear others' disapproval. We fear we are not acceptable. I should have been better. I don't measure up. I lack. What will they think of me?

This can cause us to have different ways of measuring ourselves. One is our measuring stick we use to compare ourselves with the 'should, ought to be, person' that we have created and are striving to become, usually so we and others will think well of us.

Another measuring device we use is more like a barometer which moves according to a subjective assessment of ourselves in relation to others and events. A compliment makes us feel great – a criticism is crushing. An introspective re-run of conversations and meetings working out whether we were enough, didn't say too much, said the wrong thing, looked wrong. This device records how well we think others have received us.

Both of these measuring devices must be smashed. We are meant to be the thermostat that sets the climate. We must stop listening to the lies that distort and confuse us and start listening to God's healing word that transforms us.

When we worry about what others think, we try to be what we think others want us to be. We are compliant – desperate to fit in. We try to buy love by our good deeds. A used abused somebody who fits in somewhere, rather than a nobody who belongs nowhere. We are people pleasers – doormats – volunteering for menial tasks and spiritualizing this. We allow others to take advantage of us whilst becoming more and more dissatisfied with ourselves and/or cross with others.[54]

As I have written, we grade ourselves, often against the non-existent person or the imagined expectations of others and reject parts of ourselves. We are like puppets on a string dancing to someone else's tune or playing a part in someone else's script. God doesn't want us imprisoned in the place of unrest. We need to stop trying to vindicate ourselves and realise there is no need to buy God's love or others' friendship.

STEP 2 – Stop trying to be perfect

We can believe Christianity is a self-improvement programme. When we don't accept ourselves, some 'self-help', 'how to' books become another burden to us no matter how well intended. I had to give away all my Christian 'how to' books because through my lens of non-acceptance they were just further evidence of how I failed to be the 'praying mother' or 'effective evangelist'.

They can subtly cause us to put value in what we do rather than who we are. And, of course, a self-improvement plan is exactly what it is, 'self'. We are self-sufficient, trying to improve ourselves to become acceptable and we forget God precedes us. God always has the initiative. Our efforts need to be in response to the grace offered. Jesus goes ahead of us and creates a space for us to indwell, so we begin to answer the invitation and discover God is present and active every step of the way. The pillar of fire in the desert never failed. It was not there as a result of any strength, ability or improvement in the children of Israel. Our part is to stop living as though we are alone in our struggles or difficulties. Nor are we to become fixated on how God is going to bring His answers.

So much of perfectionism is linked to control. It is fear based. We try to create a comfort zone where we believe we have everything organised so we are safe from failure and being known, and we are in control.

A friend of mine was praying for a prodigal son saying, "I have done everything I can, I've done everything I can think of. I have done the very best I can." And God said, "But you didn't get out of my way."

Control means we don't really trust God, so we must do the best we can for our family, friends and ourselves. We believe we have the experience, we know what the best is, what should be done, and we know how to make it happen.

The disciples tried to control who Jesus could and couldn't see. Shooing people and children away, like the poorly trained receptionist in the GP centre. Control is often based in fear, thinking you have to organise everything. It leads to distorted thinking like: "My way is the right way. If I am in control nothing will go wrong." It means you have to sort everything and everyone out, trying to create order on the outside to avoid the out-of-control fear feelings on the inside.

God says in Jeremiah 17:7 (TLB), *"But blessed is the man who trusts in the Lord and has made the Lord his hope and confidence. He is like a tree planted along a river bank, roots reaching deep in the water, not bothered by heat or drought. Leaves stay green with fruit."*

If perfectionism doesn't drive us to continually control everything, it can paralyze us. We exist by always putting life on hold until the conditions are perfect. Then we experience the constant disappointment of missing out because the time was never quite right.

Perfectionism is a life of 'oughts' and 'shoulds'. I should have been better, done better. I don't measure up. We judge ourselves, reject ourselves, condemn ourselves. We have a distorted self-image which drives us towards performance. We need to stop listening to the enemy's lies and learn to listen to God's accepting words.

Passive, paralyzing perfectionism leads us to be afraid to do things because it won't be perfect. We miss out on the good of making decisions. All the dreams we didn't follow because of a deep fear of failing, making a mistake, disappointing others. When we feel 'less than', we become focused on trying to be perfect but it traps us in loneliness, for satisfying relationships can only be built on honesty and total acceptance. There is no intimacy because we hide and are not authentic.

When we are obsessed with trying to be perfect, we see all our shortcomings as something to hide. Perfectionism will keep us fixated on who we are going to be someday, instead of enjoying who we are now. It causes us to be focused on self.

Perfectionism is not the same as striving to do your best. Healthy achievement is great. Perfectionism is believing the lie that if we live, look, act perfect, we will minimise or avoid the pain, blame, judgment and shame! I did everything, now it's gone wrong but it's not my fault!

Perfectionism means we try to earn approval and acceptance through self-improvement – how can I improve? Perfectionism is what must I do to please, perform, be perfect so you think well of me. Ultimately, perfection is shame based.

We can only do the best we can. We need to stop self-blaming and not identify or exaggerate our feelings: "It's a disaster." "I was horrified." "It's the worst decision I have ever made." "I'll live to regret it to my dying day."

Learn to live with imperfection. Some of the lyrics from Leonard Cohen's "Anthem" illustrate this well:

"Ring the bells that still can ring;
Forget your perfect offering;
There is a crack, a crack in everything.
That's how the light gets in."

Pursuing perfection is destructive because there is no such thing as perfect. We just become more discontent with life and ourselves.

G K Chesterton: *"If a thing is worth doing it is worth doing badly."* Sometimes, to break through into a place of rest and self-acceptance, we need to practise this.

A friend was saying how someone had given her a beautiful gift and she wanted to send a thank you note but the cards she had weren't quite right, didn't perfectly match the gift sender. So she delayed whilst looking for the perfect card. Six weeks later, she still hadn't sent a card.

Give up trying to be a saint; it is much better for everyone.

STEP 3 – Stop comparing yourself

'Go Compare' may be a good advertisement for car insurance but it is a very bad mantra for us. Comparing in families is so familiar it often goes unnoticed.

It may be overt in sentences like, "You're not like your brother John," or "I can't understand why you won't do this like your sister," or "Everyone else in the family likes/is happy with…," or "You're the only one in this family who wanted to do that." Or it can be confusing. I was told I was, 'just like my Aunty Flo,' but I didn't know what she was like.

Or it can be covert. One of the reasons I struggled with self-acceptance was because I was different from the rest of my family. For a start, I realise now I am an introvert. This doesn't and didn't mean I was shy or antisocial but I liked time on my own and was often misunderstood. Why can't you go and play with your sister, etc. Play out in the street with the other children. I preferred reading. Now part of this was unhealed wounds, a lost child preferring my fantasy world, but another part was my more creative, imaginative way of thinking. This was considered weird. As an adult I was trying to get my mother to speak more about something and she said, "All these questions – you always were a funny little thing."

Isaiah 45:9 (NLT): "What sorrow awaits those who argue with their creator. Does a clay pot argue with its maker? Does the clay pot dispute with the one who shapes it saying, 'Stop, you're doing it wrong!' Does the pot exclaim, 'How clumsy can you be?'"

Whilst meditating on this I had a picture of a potter's shed. Inside was a shelf with a row of plain white milk jugs. On the potter's wheel was a teapot which the potter was decorating. The teapot looked up at the milk jugs, looked down at its spout; then after looking again and seeing they were plain while the teapot not only had a spout but also had decoration, threw itself off the potter's wheel. That is what we do when we compare ourselves unfavourably with others.

Or we compare our marriages or partner's lives to others believing they have it easier or better. Social media cause us to compare the shiny presentation of others to our inside discontent.

STEP 4 – Stop focusing on what you don't like about yourself

Francis McNutt, a catholic priest with a healing ministry, tells the story of a priest with an injured, bad eye which distorted his appearance. After a term away at college, Francis McNutt returned and the priest's face looked different. On being asked about his changed appearance, the priest explained he had 'forgiven' his eye and accepted how he looked.

This happened to me once at a much more superficial level. I was on a cruise and I had an eye infection. This particular evening was the formal 'dress up' event. I had decided as well as the eye infection, my hair was too short and my dress made me look fat. I confessed self-hatred and asked God to help me. I got ready, looked in the mirror and decided I looked good enough. The next day I woke up and introspection started (another sign of a lack of self-acceptance) and I decided I had made it all up – God doesn't care that much that my prayer altered how I felt and therefore how I looked. My reading that morning was James 1:23, "Anyone who listens to the word but does not do what it says is like a man who looks at his face in the mirror and, after looking at himself, goes away and immediately forgets what he looks like."

However, "How do I look?" is a big struggle when we don't accept ourselves. Many of us worry about what people think of us. We have a great need to feel we are good enough and can often nurse worries and fears about what we think people think about us. Unable to tell ourselves we look okay, we continually look for external validation. "What if I don't look the part?" "What if it's clear I don't fit in?" We spend much energy trying to make ourselves who we think people want us to be, trying to look the part. When I first became a Christian, I looked very different in my choice of clothes from the other young women in the church. Within a year I found myself dressing like them. Not that I really liked the look.

This can start very early when we are not part of the cool group at school or can't manage the 'arty' look. I never could manage this, while my sister always managed it. I was praying with an amazingly good-looking girl called Hannah who was the daughter of a Baptist minister, so she had a childhood of not enough money for the 'right' clothes. As a twenty year old she started seeing a boy who used subtle criticism to control her, for instance questioning her dress sense. All the feelings of being left out, dowdy and plain came rushing back.

Media, of course, is a lot to blame. I didn't know until a few years ago I had to have a beach body. Most of the photos in advertising campaigns are enhanced (therefore unattainable for any human being). If Barbie 'the doll' was scaled up to human size, her proportions would be 36-18-33. Not helpful when we are wanting to accept ourselves.

STEP 5 – Celebrate your uniqueness

Reiterating from the previous Chapter on identity, statements like, "When God looks at us He sees Jesus," can make us feel worthless, useless and dehumanized. It is true we can neither make nor save ourselves. God does it all, but He does it because He loves what He created.

We often lack the courage to be unique because being the same as everyone else offers an element of safety.

Each of us is an original. Galatians 5:26 (MSG), *"That means we will not compare ourselves with each other as if one of us were better and another worse. We have far more interesting things to do with our lives. Each of us is an original."*

As Eugene Peterson writes in "Travelling Light": *"Each of us is an absolutely unique combination of experience and intelligence and situation. The way we live out that uniqueness cannot be assigned by another, no matter how wise or authoritative. It must be creatively worked out in our own faith responses in the Spirit. There are always some who know exactly what another is best suited for. But no one knows us well enough for that. Each of us has unique gifts, for which there are no precedents, yet which will be used in ministry. And we are quite free to resist anyone who tells us differently."*[55]

We may be surrounded by people who want to tell us what we are like, who want to make pronouncements over us, telling us what we like and don't like. It is tempting to trade our uniqueness for others' acceptance, but trying to spend our life doing and being something that is not right for us will make us uncomfortable. To accept ourselves, we need to learn to be comfortable in our own skin, at home with ourselves. Joyce Meyer says, *"Don't walk about in shoes that don't fit."*

When I first became a Christian, three of us became Christians all at once. We were all about the same age and our children had just started at school. We met at the school gate. I flourished very, very quickly. We were all in a discipleship group together, and the girl who led all three of us to the Lord asked God what was going on, because she couldn't understand the great discrepancies in the three of us. She had a picture of seeds being planted and one seed flourished very quickly into a rose tree with lots of roses on it. Another one became a beautiful orchid that needed to go into a greenhouse, and the third one was a sapling growing into an oak tree and needed a lot of support to begin with. She just told us the story, but I knew, although she didn't say it, that I was the rose tree and I tried to pull off my roses because I felt guilty beside the sapling and I thought I was meant to be weak at this point too.

This is so what we are like. The problem was none of us really understood or appreciated what was going on. If we are busy comparing the weedy stick with the orchid that's got to go into the greenhouse with the rose bush that's flourishing, we get thoroughly confused and don't appreciate that, as we are actually meant to be different, unique; our route to 'becoming' may well be equally different. So we try to make ourselves like someone else – like the orchid or whatever. This is foolishness, the real foolishness of comparing ourselves to one another. We don't even understand we are judging the unseen. We have no idea what God is doing, and what's worse, we don't trust that He does know what He is doing! There never has been and never will be another you.

STEP 6 – Know you are eligible

Shrinking in a corner,
pressed into a wall;
do they know I'm present,
am I here at all?

Is there a written rule book,
that tells you how to be –
all the right things to talk about –
That everyone has but me?

Slowly I am withering –
a flower deprived of sun;
longing to belong to –
somewhere or someone.

Lang Leav[56]

Ephesians 2:16-20 (MSG): *"Christ brought us together through his death on the cross. The Cross got us to embrace, and that was the end of the hostility. Christ came and preached peace to you outsiders and peace to us insiders. He treated us as equals, and so made us equals. Through him we both share the same Spirit and have equal access to the Father.*

"That's plain enough, isn't it? You're no longer wandering exiles. This kingdom of faith is now your home country. You're no longer strangers or outsiders. You belong here, with as much right to the name Christian as anyone. God is building a home…"

There are few joys in life like being wanted, chosen, embraced. There are few pains like being excluded, rejected, left out. We are all eligible because Jesus comes to bind up the broken hearted, to heal the sick, to set us free. We come to Jesus who wants to enter into our wounds, so no-one is too broken, too traumatised, too unworthy, to belong. *"The sense of belonging is the sense of human being."* (Desmond Tutu)

When we don't think we are eligible, don't accept ourselves, we don't want to be known. We want to be invisible or just present the part of ourselves we find acceptable. The more successful we are at this, the more we feel overlooked, not eligible, and then reject more of ourselves, remaining on the outside, unknown.

"Being unwanted, unloved, uncared for, forgotten by everybody, I think that is a much greater hunger, a much greater poverty than the person who has nothing to eat." (Mother Teresa)

If we spend honest time with God, He will teach us how to spend honest time with others. We need to get to a place wherein our 'everyday, ordinary' Christianity is lived from a place of rest. We have the confidence to know that belonging is part of our destiny, our inheritance. When we don't accept or approve of ourselves, we project this onto God and think He doesn't accept us. We believe ourselves not eligible.

Philippians 3:3 (NLT): *"We rely on what Christ Jesus has done for us. We put no confidence in human effort."* No human effort! When we fear that we are not acceptable to God and to others we are always trying harder. We never believe we are (good) enough – either for God, for ourselves or for others. We don't like ourselves and do not believe God likes us. We do not know who we are in Christ and feel unworthy in a negative, self-rejecting way. To an extent there is some pride in us because, in essence, we are saying Christ's broken body on the cross – causing the temple veil to be torn apart, opening the way to the Holy of Holies – is not enough! We are saying that unless we do more, strive, etc, God is not welcoming of us.

We can have a shame-based, self-rejecting identity, ashamed of ourselves, and therefore present a phony, false personality. We need to learn to look in the right mirror. We need to learn to get along with ourselves. When we fear being unacceptable to God we strive – praying, memorising, reading the Bible, etc, to keep God happy, to make Him like us. We are completely missing the relationship. We are doing it for the wrong reason. We are trying to BUY love, not believing ourselves eligible.

The destructiveness of the 'not eligible' mentality is well illustrated in the case of the 'non-dancers', a group observed by Pierre Bourdieu, a French anthropologist. These 'non-dancers' were lonely thirty-something men on the edge of the dance floor at village events in 1950s France. They did not join the fun because, as elder brothers who had inherited the family farm, they were tied to the land and had not acquired city ways, unlike their younger brothers. Lacking the ability to jive, these bachelor farmers classified themselves as unappealing to women and thus condemned themselves to be unmarriageable.

Our slave-like, non-eligible mental attitude can be a self-constructed prison which excludes us from the rest Jesus has offered us. We are all familiar with the picture of a caged bird with an open door, but the bird doesn't fly out. This may be fear, wanting to stay in the familiar prison but sometimes, in picture language, we do not believe we are eligible to join with others in flying because we believe the lie that we have clipped wings.

When we have experienced a rigid, controlling childhood, we are not given permission to fly. So we 'look at our wings' frustrated with ourselves. What are they? What's the point of them? I haven't got what it takes to join. If we have come from a family without boundaries, we may have experimented with life, got it wrong and been damaged. We then believe the wings are the problem and start not liking ourselves, not accepting ourselves, ineligible to join 'the flying club'.

I know I have written on this verse before, but it is such a good illustration of the children of Israel's inability to accept themselves and know they are eligible for all that God has provided for them. This verse is the report of ten of the spies sent to look at the land. Joshua and Caleb report that it is indeed a land flowing with milk and honey and although well-fortified, they should enter and occupy it for, "*We are well able to overcome it*". (Numbers 13:30)

However, the other ten report the giants in the land and then say, "*We felt like grasshoppers next to them and that's what we looked like to them.*" (Numbers 13:33)

Despite all that God had done in delivering them from Egypt, they still had a slave mentality. Unable to accept themselves they saw themselves as grasshoppers – not as the children of God – and projected this onto the occupants of the land – "and so we seemed to them". When we have this unhealed view of ourselves and we believe we are 'less than', we see everything through this lens.

I was speaking to someone in church about her experiences of being ignored in a rather smart London store. I said, "I know, the service there is appalling." She said, "Have you had that trouble?" I said something like, "You get better service in the local supermarket." I then realised she had interpreted her experience through the lens of 'I am not eligible to be here. I don't look smart enough, etc.'

I suffered from feelings of not being eligible, 'not fitting in', for many years. Partly because I think there was a spiritual component to this, in that my father was illegitimate but there was also the hidden script of his orphaned heart. One story that illustrates this well is when I was a trustee of Living Waters and along with Andy Comiskey, founder of Desert Stream, was the main speaker at a three-day conference. On arrival at the church on the first morning, I walked round the back of the stage and one door read 'Welcome Team' and the other door 'London Team'. I thought that I didn't belong to either of those, so went and sat down on the second row, ready for the conference to begin. When it was my time to speak, I went on the platform and taught. I noticed that the two organisers of the conference and Andy were sitting on the stage with an empty chair, but I took no notice.

I went to lunch on my own and came home about 10.00 that evening on my own. The next morning, one of the organisers came to find me and asked if I preferred sitting in the second row rather than on the platform, and did I prefer to eat alone rather than joining in the team room, and did I not arrive early enough for the prayer in the 'London Team' room? I had no idea I was included. And of course, to them, I probably appeared aloof and 'stand-offish'.

One man came to see me for prayer who felt very insecure in male company. In prayer, this is the picture he had: "I am standing in the basement of a department store where there are returned and defective goods. Jesus is standing by the escalator inviting me to go up to the next floor. I step on the escalator but realise I cannot stay on the next floor because I have the wrong currency in my pocket." He believed the lie he didn't have 'what it takes'. Not eligible.

One last picture: I was at a leaders' prayer meeting where we were praying for the last evening's celebration following a five-day conference. There were lots of words and pictures about a wonderful party/banquet. None of which was wrong, but I had a different picture. I saw this party taking place on a large cruise liner and when I looked there were quite a lot of people on the quayside. I left the ship to find out why they hadn't come on board for the party. They all had invitations in their hands. Some were asking, "How much does it cost?", with the inference, "I can't afford it". Others, seeing the splendour of the ship, had concluded the invite had been sent to the wrong address!

Contrast this with a story of a young man who is able to accept himself. Ben was vision impaired, had suffered a stroke and had various other physical difficulties. On entering senior school age 11, all the children were asked to write something of their story. Ben entitled his, "My Life – Laughter and Tears". He wrote about his cat dying, included some pictures of himself in hospital and finished with this, "I like myself. I know I am a little odd but then so is everyone else."

I wrote this in my prayer journal, "Truth comes whispering – you don't have to be imprisoned – you can see, you can hear, you can have wisdom. When the Holy Spirit of truth covers our hearts, that freedom burns off the lies that imprison our souls."

PRAYER

Father,

I confess my envy, comparison and my sinful ability to measure myself, introspect and hide.

I want to be unwrapped. Please help me, and help me to allow others to be part of the process of my self-acceptance. Amen.

Chapter 6

WHAT'S IN A NAME?

In the beginning, God spoke into the nothingness, the void, the bottomless emptiness. God speaks a name 'light', and that name 'light' fills the space.

Adam's first task is to name the creatures, thus continuing the creation plan. Naming is part of the language of love – a kingdom principle.

Father Schmemann writes, "*Now in the Bible, a name reveals the very essence of a thing, or rather its essence as God's gift. To name a thing is to manifest the meaning and value God gave it, to know it as coming from God and to know its place and function within the cosmos created by God. To name a thing, in other words, is to bless God for it and in it.*"[57]

In order to live in rest, we need to know what we were created for, where we come from and where we are going. This is why the TV programme, "Who Do You Think You Are?" is so clever. It explores people's ancestry, linking past connection to identity.

A name is not just a label. It is linked to who you are. We find our face, being and identity in listening to God and letting Him name us.

Often in life we have different names in different circumstances. You may have changed your name on marrying, divorcing, marrying again. We may be called Miss, Sir, Teacher, Boss, Mum, Bruv, Sis, Dad, Nana, Grandad. Or perhaps we also have a pet name that only certain people are allowed to use.

John 10:3 (TLB): *"The sheep hear his voice and come to him; and he calls his own sheep by name."*

Isaiah 43:1: *"Do not fear for I have redeemed you. I have called you by name."*

At birth we are named, not numbered. To be called by name is part of the process of becoming our true self. Any time we move from personal names to abstract labels or graphs, something dehumanising is happening.

At my local health centre when I ring, the first thing the receptionist (and therefore the computer) wants is my date of birth, not my name. In prisons and in the armed forces everyone is given a number. There is a need for uniformity, not uniqueness.

Names call us to become who we will be; they call us to become what we are not yet. It is in relationship with God we are named. Eugene Peterson writes, "Naming is a way of hoping and fulfilling our uniqueness."[58]

Naming gives us value. We don't call a dog, 'dog' or a cat, 'cat', even though they are just as likely to respond.

I gave a friend of mine who likes ducks, a wooden duck for her conservatory. Her grandchildren were there so she said to them, "What shall we name the duck?" The four year old said, 'Donald', which was considered lacking in imagination by his older sister who announced the duck's name was Jennifer. So, many years later, this wooden ornament is still referred to as Jennifer.

How would you feel if God didn't know your name? Or if a teacher never knows your name but calls you, "You in the third row."

In the junior school I went to, we were all called by our surname. My maiden name was Evans and there were two other pupils with the same surname – one being my sister. I was the eldest of the three, so I was called 'Big Evans', the other girl 'Little Evans' and my sister by her Christian name, 'Sandra'! Not a good recipe for making you feel good about yourself.

In the ancient Hebraic mindset, to name someone is to give them existence, purpose and function. Which is why in the Bible God sometimes changes names to reflect a new purpose of calling, but we also see this in political life. A quick check on the internet shows many examples.

In Prague, the square in front of the Russian Embassy was re-named Boris Nemtsov Square after a critic of the Russian government who was murdered in 2015. Also in Prague in 2022, a part of the street used by the Russian Embassy was re-named Heroes of Ukraine. In Glasgow in 1986, a street adjoining the South African Embassy was re-named Nelson Mandela Place. Sometimes cities are re-named. St Petersburg was renamed Leningrad then Stalingrad then back to St Petersburg. We have all adapted recently in changing how we spell the Ukrainian capital. Kiev comes from the Russian language, Kyiv from the Ukrainian language. On a lighter note, in Edinburgh there is Costkea Way named after the resident stores IKEA and Costco. In Leicester, Lineker Road is named after the famous footballer.

So back to the Bible, where names have deep significance and were carefully chosen to have meaning and purpose. There are many times in the Bible when a person's name was changed, or a nickname is given. Not all these names came from God, but all name changes marked a transformation in the people who were renamed. Here are eight examples:

Abram/Abraham (Genesis 17:1-5)
God appeared to Abram when he was 99 years old and made a promise to bless Abram and multiply his descendants. God then changed his name from Abram (meaning "exalted father") to Abraham (meaning "father of a multitude").

Sarai/Sarah (Genesis 17:15)
In the same conversation where God changed Abram's name, He also changed his wife's name from Sarai to Sarah. Both names mean "Princess", but the change marks a new season in Sarai's life as God works through her as well.

Jacob/Israel (Genesis 32:38)
After an overnight wrestle with God, Jacob's name (meaning "supplanter") was changed to Israel (meaning "He strives with God") and a blessing was bestowed on Jacob.

Joseph/Zaphenath-paneah (Genesis 41:45)
Pharoah was so impressed by Joseph, he gave him a new Egyptian name, Zaphenath-paneah, along with a wife.

Hoshea/Joshua (Numbers 13:16)
At his first task of leading the spies in scoping out the Promised Land, Hoshea ("salvation") becomes Joshua ('Yahweh saves') at Moses' direction.

Naomi/Mara (Ruth 1:20) negatively renames herself;
On return to her homeland without her husband and sons, Naomi tells those who excitedly greet her that she should no longer be called Naomi ('pleasant'), but Mara ('bitter').

Daniel, Hananiah, Mishael and Azariah/Belteshazzar, Shadrach, Meshach and Abednego (Daniel 1:7)
When Daniel and his friends were taken as captives into Babylon, they were designated new names by the chief official as a way to force their assimilation into Babylonian culture.

Simon/Peter (John 1:42)
Jesus gives His disciple Simon (meaning one who 'hears') a new name in Peter which means 'rock'. At the time, this name seems strange as Simon Peter's character does not seem reflective or worthy of this moniker, but he really grows into it as he continues Jesus' ministry on earth after the crucifixion.

God can also give us new names if we ask, sometimes calling into being that which isn't yet.

Romans 4:17 (TLB): *"This is what the scriptures mean when they say God made Abraham the father of many nations. God will accept all people in every nation who trust God as Abraham did. And this promise is from God himself who makes the dead live again and speaks of future events with as much certainty as though they were already past."*

When I first asked God for a new name, He said I had been named correctly, Linda (meaning beautiful). Several years later God added the name Sophia (meaning wisdom). And then last year at the New Wine Leaders' Conference in Harrogate, the person on the platform said, "God is making a cake with different ingredients." I asked God, "What am I?" and He said, "Sultana". On returning home, I looked up the meaning, which said it was feminine and meant strength and authority. It was related to spiritual leadership, not political. This was extremely meaningful at the time concerning a decision I needed to take.

Revelation 2:17 (TPT): *"But the one whose heart is open, let him listen carefully to what the Spirit is presently saying to all the churches. To everyone who is victorious I will let him feast on the hidden manna and give him a shining white stone. And written upon the white stone is inscribed his new name, known only to the one who receives it."*

The imagery is amazing. In ancient times, the Romans awarded a white stone to a person on trial who was acquitted. White stones were given, with their name on, to winners of the Olympic Games. Invitations to weddings and banquets were given on white stones. So, we are forgiven, more than conquerors and invited to the eternal wedding feast/banquet.

We are, of course, also given a new name when we are adopted. Our new name, or the name God confirms, is evidence we are a member of God's family. The giving of the white stone with the new name is the communication of what God thinks about us.

The true name is one which expresses the character, the nature, the meaning of the person who bears it. It is the man's own symbol – his soul's picture in a word – the sign which belongs to him and to no-one else. God alone names us. God sees our potential from the beginning and names us. He had this in mind when he began to create us. He kept this in His thought through the long process of our becoming.

Each man has his individual relation to God, his unique relation to God. He is to God a unique being, made after his own fashion, and that of no-one else.

For each, God has a different response. With every man He has a secret – the secret of a new name. I believe there is a room in God's heart with our name on it. No-one but us can enter this room. This place in God's heart is where we find our rest.

The following story retold by John Shea in "Starlight: Beholding the Christmas Miracle All Year Long" encapsulates much of what I have tried to convey in this book.

Starlight by John Shea

'The story is told of a very pious Jewish couple. They had married with great love, and the love never died. Their greatest hope was to have a child so their love could walk the earth with joy.

Yet there were difficulties. And since they were very pious, they prayed and prayed and prayed. Along with considerable other efforts, lo and behold, the wife conceived. When she conceived, she laughed louder than Sarah laughed when she conceived Isaac. And the child leapt in her womb more joyously than John leapt in the womb of Elizabeth when Mary visited her. And nine months later a delightful little boy came rumbling into the world.

They named him Mordecai. He was rambunctious, zestful, gulping down the days and dreaming through the nights. The sun and the moon were his toys. He grew in age and wisdom and grace, until it was time to go to the synagogue and learn the Word of God.

The night before his studies were to begin, his parents sat Mordecai down and told him how important the Word of God was. They stressed that without the Word of God Mordecai would be an autumn leaf in the winter's wind. He listened wide-eyed. Yet the next day he never arrived at the synagogue. Instead, he found himself in the woods, swimming in the lake and climbing the trees.

When he came home that night, the news had spread throughout the small village. Everyone knew his shame. His parents were beside themselves. They did not know what to do.

So they called in the behaviour modificators to modify Mordecai's behaviour, until there was no behaviour of Mordecai that was not modified. Nevertheless, the next day he found himself in the woods, swimming in the lake and climbing the trees.

So they called in the psychoanalysts, who unblocked Mordecai's blockages, so there were no more blocks for Mordecai to be blocked by. Nevertheless, he found himself the next day, swimming in the lake and climbing trees.
His parents grieved for their beloved son. There seemed to be no hope.

At this same time the Great Rabbi visited the village. And the parents said, "Ah! Perhaps the 'Rabbi.'" So they took Mordecai to the Rabbi and told him their tale of woe. The Rabbi bellowed, "Leave the boy with me, and I will have a talking with him."

It was bad enough that Mordecai would not go to the synagogue. But to leave their beloved son alone with this lion of a man was terrifying. However, they had come this far, and so they left him.

Now Mordecai stood in the hallway, and the Great Rabbi stood in his parlour. He beckoned, "Boy, come here." Trembling, Mordecai came forward.

And the Great Rabbi picked him up and held him silently against his heart.

His parents came to get Mordecai, and they took him home. The next day he went to the synagogue to learn the Word of God. And when he was done, he went to the woods. And the Word of God became one with the words of the woods, which became one with the words of Mordecai. And he swam in the lake. And the Word of God became one with the words of the lake, which became one with the words of Mordecai. And he climbed trees. And the Word of God became one with the words of the trees, which became one with the words of Mordecai.

And Mordecai himself grew up to become a great man. People who were seized with panic came to him and found peace. People who were without anybody came to him and found communion. People with no exits came to him and found a way. And when they came to him, he said, "I first learned the Word of God when the Great Rabbi held me silently against his heart."'

EPILOGUE

In this book, I have attempted to look at rest not so much from the position of life-style changes, but more the internal changes that take place when we are able to practice the presence of Jesus.

In Chapter one, I explored how rest is more than having time off from our daily commitments. What we need is a transformation of our hearts to truly experience rest and peace. Even with outward busyness, we can 'go slow' on the inside.

The difficulty of writing a book is the necessity to divide subjects into Chapters. Our lives are not like that, but what I wanted to illustrate in Chapter two is how our experiences impact how we see ourselves and God. We are shaped and motivated by family, friends and church. This affects our relationship with God.

Chapters three and four, the core of the book, are about being able to lay our head on Jesus' chest and listen to the heartbeat of God. However, because of our orphan mentality, even then we have to struggle with our 'rest robbers' – our identity and not really knowing 'who we are'. This makes it a challenge to live in God's love. Still striving because we doubt our inheritance, we are unable to rest in the goodness of God.

In Chapter five, I wrote that a lack of self-acceptance robs us of our rest: not comfortable with ourselves, not at home within ourselves – tiring ourselves by judging and measuring ourselves. It is not enough to know God accepts us unless we accept ourselves in Him.

And then Chapter six, the power of being named. I am not a number, a statistic, a slave. I am named by God who sees me and wants me to celebrate my uniqueness in a relationship with Him.

Recently, when someone was commenting on my busy schedule, I found myself replying that though I was busy, internally, I was at rest. So, I am praying that those of you who began this book with the question, "Can I be at rest when I am busy?", having read the book, will be able to answer, "Yes".

END NOTES

1.   Tim Keller *King's Cross*

2.   Tim Keller *King's Cross*

3.   For more insight and information see Maurice Balme *Attitudes to Work and Desire in Ancient Greece* and Josef Pieper *Leisure, the Basis of Culture*

4.   Dr Stuart Brown *Play: How it Shapes the Brain, Opens the Imagination and Invigorates the Soul*

5.   Brené Brown *The Gifts of Imperfection*

6.   McLean Ministries

7.   Quoted by John Mark Comer in his book *The Ruthless Elimination of Hurry*

8.   Walter Adams was C S Lewis' spiritual director

9.   John Ortberg *Soul Keeping — Caring for the Most Important Part of You*

10.   Jack Frost's *Experiencing the Father's Embrace* has more on this.

11.   Lin Button *Father Matters*

12.   Robert Karen *Becoming Attached, First Relationships and How They Shape Our Capacity to Love*

13.   Lin Button *Sorry Matters* Chapter 5, 'Hiding'

14.   Lynne Twist *The Soul of Money*

15.   C S Lewis *Mere Christianity*

16.   C S Lewis *Mere Christianity*

END NOTES (continued)

17.   Patrick Carnes *Recovery Start Kit*

18.   Josef Pieper *Faith, Hope and Love*

19.   Josef Pieper *Faith, Hope and Love*

20.   C S Lewis *Mere Christianity*

21.   Jonathan Merritt *Jesus is Better than You Imagined*

22.   Gerald Sittser *Water from a Deep Well*

23.   Nicky Gumbel Commentary *The Bible in One Year*

24.   C S Lewis *Letters to Malcolm, Chiefly on Prayer*

25.   Susan S Phillips *The Cultivated Life*

26.   Gerard Hughes *God of Surprises*

27.   The 'Father Christmas' image is from Brad Jersak *A More Christlike God*

28.   Brad Jersak *A More Christlike God*

29.   Google search: Bible verse melted to steel in 9/11 attacks

30.   Quoted from Thomas Merton *Contemplative Critic*

31.   Dallas Willard *The Spirit of the Disciplines: Understanding How God Changes Lives*

32.   C S Lewis *The Weight of Glory*

33.   Henri Nouwen *The Return of the Prodigal Son*

34.   Brennan Manning *The Ragamuffin Gospel*

35.   Book of Common Prayer 1662, "From all the deceits of the world, the flesh and the devil, Good Lord, deliver us."

36.   Leon D Thomassian in an article in *The Atlantic Union Cleaner* October 2015

37.   Eugene Peterson *Reversed Thunder*

38.   John Stott *The Contemporary Christian – an urgent plea for double listening*

39.   Dietrich Bonhoeffer *Life Together*

40.   I first started thinking about this when I read Brennan Manning's *The Ragamuffin Gospel*

41.   C S Lewis The Lion, the Witch and the Wardrobe

42.   John Eldredge *Waking the Dead*

43.   See Lin Button *Sorry Matters*

44.   See also Jack Frost's book *Spiritual Slavery to Spiritual Sonship*

45.   'Treatise on Christian Liberty' quoted by A Voskamp *The Broken Way*

46.   Dr Pamela Evans *Driven Beyond the Call of God*

47.   Dr Pamela Evans *Driven Beyond the Call of God*

48.   C S Lewis *Letters to Malcolm, chiefly on Prayer*

49.   Thomas Merton *Seeds of Contemplation*

50.   Paraphrase of Leanne Payne from *The Broken Image*

51.   C S Lewis *Mere Christianity*

END NOTES (continued)

52.   Leanne Payne excerpts from *Restoring the Christian Soul*

53.   This is based on listening to a Joyce Meyer teaching

54.   There is more on this in *Father Matters* Lin Button

55.   Eugene Peterson *Travelling Light*

56.   Lang Leav *Love and Misadventure*

57.   Alexandre Schmemann *For the Life of the World: Sacraments and Orthodoxy*

58.   Eugene Peterson *The Quest*

Other titles by Lin Button:

Mother Matters
Father Matters
Sorry Matters
Ordinary Matters

These are available via the website, along with further resources and information:
www.healingprayerschool.org.uk